W9-BIN-328

# HEALING
*for a* WOMAN'S
# EMOTIONS

# HEALING
*for a* WOMAN'S
# EMOTIONS

## PAULA SANDFORD

**Charisma**
**HOUSE**
A STRANG COMPANY

Most STRANG COMMUNICATIONS/CHARISMA HOUSE/SILOAM/
FRONTLINE/REALMS products are available at special quantity
discounts for bulk purchase for sales promotions, premiums,
fund-raising, and educational needs. For details, write Strang
Communications/Charisma House/Siloam/FrontLine/Realms,
600 Rinehart Road, Lake Mary, Florida 32746, or telephone (407)
333-0600.

HEALING FOR A WOMAN'S EMOTIONS by Paula Sandford
Published by Charisma House
A Strang Company
600 Rinehart Road
Lake Mary, Florida 32746
www.charismahouse.com

This book or parts thereof may not be reproduced in any form,
stored in a retrieval system, or transmitted in any form by
any means—electronic, mechanical, photocopy, recording, or
otherwise—without prior written permission of the publisher,
except as provided by United States of America copyright law.

Unless otherwise noted, all Scripture quotations are from the New
American Standard Bible. Copyright © 1960, 1962, 1963, 1968,
1971, 1972, 1973, 1975, 1977 by the Lockman Foundation. Used by
permission. (www.Lockman.org)

Scripture quotations marked AMP are from the Amplified
Bible. Old Testament copyright © 1965, 1987 by the Zondervan
Corporation. The Amplified New Testament copyright © 1954,
1958, 1987 by the Lockman Foundation. Used by permission.

Scripture quotations marked KJV are from the King James Version
of the Bible.

Scripture quotations marked NIV are from the Holy Bible, New
International Version. Copyright © 1973, 1978, 1984, International
Bible Society. Used by permission.

Scripture quotations marked NKJV are from the New King James Version of the Bible. Copyright © 1979, 1980, 1982 by Thomas Nelson, Inc., publishers. Used by permission.

Scripture quotations marked RSV are from the Revised Standard Version of the Bible. Copyright © 1946, 1952, 1971 by the Division of Christian Education of the National Council of the Churches of Christ in the USA. Used by permission.

Cover design by Rafael Sabino

Copyright © 2007 by Paula Sandford
All rights reserved

Library of Congress Cataloging-in-Publication Data
Sandford, Paula.
  [Healing women's emotions]
  Healing for a woman's emotions / Paula Sandford.
      p. cm.
  Reprint. Originally published: Healing women's emotions. Tulsa, Okla. : Victory House, c1992.
  Includes bibliographical references.
  ISBN-13: 978-1-59979-054-1 (trade paper) 1. Christian women--Religious life. 2. Emotions--Religious aspects--Christianity.
  I. Title.
  BV4527.S24 2007
  248.8'43--dc22
                          2006030534

This book was previously published as *Healing Women's Emotions* by Victory House, Inc., copyright © 1992, ISBN 0-932081-30-4.

07 08 09 10 11 — 987654321
Printed in the United States of America

*This book is lovingly dedicated to my husband, John.*

# CONTENTS

# FOREWORD

MANY PEOPLE, WOMEN ESPECIALLY, are walking around with wounded souls, searching for a place of peace where they can find rest and healing. As women, God created us to be more emotional than men, and we experience those emotions more deeply than men do. There is nothing wrong with allowing yourself to feel those emotions, but when you become bound in your pain from emotional woundedness, sometimes you have no clue where to turn for help.

Sadly, many are looking in the wrong places for that peace. Some resort to false doctrines or religions such as New Age, Kabbalah, Wicca, or other sources. Women are turning to antianxiety and antidepressant medications, which often act as bandages and allow them to function "normally" in their everyday life, but, in reality, they live on the ragged edge.

As believers in Jesus Christ, however, we know there are answers through the power of the Holy Spirit that will heal the soul. The only one with the supernatural power to heal the mind, will, and emotions is Jesus, the Savior of the world.

Psalm 23:1–3 gives us a very strong declaration for healing our wounded souls. "The Lord is my shepherd; *I shall not want.* He makes me to lie down in green pastures; He leads me beside the still waters. *He restores my soul*" (emphasis added, NKJV).

There is a powerful truth in those two phrases: "I shall not want" and "He restores my soul." In the first phrase, the words *shall want* are derived from the Hebrew *chacer*, which means "to lack; to fail." If you are wounded in your soul today, know that the Good Shepherd will fill the void if you allow Him, and you will not want for anything. The words *He restores*, in the second phrase, come from the Hebrew *shuwb*, which means "to turn back." He wants to heal your hurts, which will cause you to turn back to a place of intimacy with Him and move you away from past wounds.

Paula Sandford, in my opinion, stands out as a giant in the kingdom and an expert in the field of restoring wounded souls. She and her husband, John, have spent their lives healing wounded souls. They know not only how to minister wholeness to each part of the person God has created us to be but also how to help us find that place of living beside still waters and green pastures.

As my prayer partner and friend, Paula has prayed for my family and me for many years. She is genuine, and her God-given insight to restore the soul is powerful and life-giving. What she teaches works!

As you read *Healing for a Woman's Emotions*, you are embarking on one of the most impacting journeys you can take in life—the journey to wholeness and peace.

Welcome to the place of still waters and green pastures!

—CINDY JACOBS
DALLAS, TEXAS

# PREFACE

I HAVE ATTEMPTED TO WRITE concerning subjects about which I am most often asked questions. I don't pretend to have all the answers, but I assure you that those I offer have been tried, tested, and lived in a practical way over a great many years. I believe they will be helpful to those who make them their own.

I have not addressed the issue of sexual abuse, although I see it as the most emotionally damaging experience a woman can endure. Charisma House will be publishing my book on this very important subject. It was previously published by Victory House, Inc., in 1988, under the title *Healing Victims of Sexual Abuse*. A great number of abuse victims have told me that it has brought them more healing than any other book they have read on the subject, and many counselors have also expressed their appreciation and recommended it to their clients.

I pray that *Healing for a Woman's Emotions* will become a blessing of insights and understandings for all women. May those understandings become tools to better enable them to handle their emotions in redemptive and constructive ways.

I also hope that men who read this book will be enlightened concerning the women with whom they live and work. And I earnestly pray that they might become better equipped to respect, cherish, nurture, and protect the mysterious gifts God has given to them—womanly gifts that will rarely fit the size and shape of man-made boxes.

—PAULA SANDFORD

# Chapter 1

# HAPPY
## *to* BE ME

I ENJOY BEING A WOMAN.

Even though I have sometimes felt frustrated or angry when confronted by double standards and ignorant, biased opinions concerning the place and value of women in our society, I have never seriously entertained jealousies of men or dreams of relinquishing who I am for any other identity. Even today, in the first decade of the twenty-first century, greater advantages in areas of job opportunity, recognition, and reward still exist in many places to the male of the species (just because he is a male), but they have never seemed to be so appealing to me that I would, if I could, exchange places with a man.

Nor would I exchange my experiences as daughter, sister, wife, mother, grandmother, or great-grandmother. Though I must admit that sometimes I don't *like* me, I have come to like *being* me. And more importantly, I have learned to *love* me, as God Himself does.

Life brings endless varieties of trials, struggles, disappointments, wounds, victories, and blessings. I have known and struggled with powerful emotions in response to all of these. Like most other people, I have spent time wallowing in feelings, stewing in self-righteousness and anger, making up speeches. I have struggled with self-condemnation for failing to live up to expectations I put upon myself. Some of my feelings have rolled verbally eloquent from an unruly tongue—and some have nearly blown a fuse inside of me.

Over the years, by the grace and loving discipline of the Lord, I have been taught redemptive ways of handling these inner fires. I have come to know and appreciate that the distinctly female sensitivities that allow me to feel emotionally devastated or driven are the *same* ones that enable me to experience the blessing to soar and sing with every part of my being. Or to carry others in my heart as I would carry a child within my womb, travailing until Christ be formed in them (Gal. 4:19).

The difference lies in what I am able to *do* with my feelings, and that is the subject of this book.

The cultural limitations put upon women will continue to change because that is part of mankind's sin and God's redemptive plan. Some of those changes may happen only as women step forward to speak out for equal opportunity and justice. But your ability to experience and participate freely in fullness of life before, as, and after *exterior* bondages and barriers have been broken depends upon the condition of your own heart. If the Lord is allowed to minister to the depths of your being, you will be healed *innerly* and set free to become all that you can be—in your home, in the church, in the marketplace, and in the world.

You will know your identity and your worth regardless of the circumstances in which you live or the yet unchanged attitudes and actions of the people with whom you are in relationship. You will be free to make decisions concerning difficult situations and oppressive relationships according to the calling and direction of the Lord. You will not be in bondage to legalisms or compulsive needs to succeed or please or belong, or to be the savior and redeemer of another person's life.

I am who I am as a gift of God. I sometimes cringe when some well-meaning individual tries to elevate and honor me by neutering me. I do not aspire to be a "chair*person*"; I am honored to be a "chair*woman*" and will attempt to be myself in any such position, with dignity, authority, common sense, skill, and sensitivity to others, that is enhanced by my sexuality, not hampered by it.

I grieve for some who fight so energetically and angrily for male privilege and recognition that they unconsciously destroy their own qualities of femininity and forfeit the greater portion of their birthright. On the other hand, I grieve even more for the woman who thinks so little of herself that she lays her glory down like a doormat in the delusion of false submission and invites a man to wipe his feet on her.

If the attitude of others toward me as a woman makes the performance of my office or expression of my identity or calling more difficult, I will still know who I am, and I receive their resistance as another exercise in forgiveness. Sometimes when my husband and I have gone out to teach, the opening session has been much more difficult for me than for him. I have keenly felt walls of resistance: "What can she, a woman, have to say to me?" Those barriers were melted down each time before our teaching was half finished, but before the breakthrough, I had to spend energy to rise above the blockage.

Many times pastors and others have graciously and humbly confessed and asked my forgiveness for having brought that sort of blocking prejudice into a meeting. Such confessions may tempt me to nurse my feelings of, "Not fair! Why should my sex be an issue? We were both invited here, but John is free to concentrate fully on teaching because he doesn't have to fight such ridiculous resistance!" On the other hand, such an opportunity may lead me to choose gratitude for a victory won.

If I were not basically secure in who I am despite what anyone thinks of me, that choice would be very difficult. Especially if no one did apologize. But insofar as I am secure, I have been able to meet and accept others where they are with no personal threat to my self-esteem and no compulsive need for self-defense.

My husband and I have been married for more than fifty-six years, and John loves to tell people that marriage is a twenty-four-hour-a-day exercise in forgiveness. We can laugh at that together now. In the early years of our marriage, our experience of "getting to know you" was often a mixture of pain and ecstasy. But today I can testify to the very practical truth of Romans 5:1–5 (emphasis added):

> Therefore having been justified by faith, we have peace with God through our Lord Jesus Christ, through whom also we have obtained our introduction by faith into this grace in which we stand; and we exult in hope of the glory of God. And not only this, but we also exult in our tribulations, knowing that tribulation brings about perseverance; and perseverance, proven character; and proven character, hope; *and hope does not disappoint, because the love of God has been poured out within our hearts* through the Holy Spirit who was given to us.

Married or single, how do you take hold of hope, peace, love, and glory in the midst of an increasingly sinful generation? If you have had a lifelong struggle from living with an alcoholic or with abusive behavior directed toward you, "we…exult in our tribulations" doesn't sound like anything but masochistic craziness. And if you have desperately wanted to love and nurture a loved one who consistently shut you out, "hope does not disappoint" seems like an empty promise.

Continually reinforced feelings of rejection may have dragged you down into a real sense of futility. Making sense of such things, and learning to live healthily with your emotions before you see any evidence of redemption in people or any change of circumstances, is what this book is about. And this book is also about healing, which means vastly more than just feeling better.

# Chapter 2

# WOMEN'S LIBERATION *in the* BIBLE

T HE QUESTION OF PROPER and acceptable roles for men and women has too long been filled with confusion, threat and hurt, emotional striving, and attack and defense. God is moving upon His church to "restore all things" (Matt. 17:11; Mark 9:12). Today, especially, we need to have a sturdy biblical foundation on which we can stand so that we can step forward to take hold of the life and good works God has prepared beforehand for us to walk in (Eph. 2:10). This is especially important as we work out our basic relationships. Let's go back to the beginning.

## GOD'S PERFECT PLAN

It is ridiculous to think that God created man and afterward found that He had forgotten something that necessitated a little addendum. Woman is in no way a postscript. God knew *from the beginning* that it was not good for man to be alone.

> And the LORD God said, It is not good that the man should
> be alone; I will make him an help meet for him.
>
> —GENESIS 2:18, KJV

It is important to note here that the word *helpmeet* means "a power equal to man." *Equal* power does not necessarily mean *same* power. Some versions of the Bible use the word *helper*. But understand that the female "helper" that God provides for man from his rib (the area of his heart) is intended to be a helpmeet, one who is designed to *meet* her husband. She is not just an incidental, though helpful, appendage, and certainly not inferior in quality or value.

It was not good for man to be alone. God created woman with the preplanned intent that she and the man would complement, bless, nurture, and upbuild one another. His plan for their duality was His best hope and device for the fullness of their maturation, so that He might have fellowship with His growing children.

> And the man said, "This is now bone of my bones, and
> flesh of my flesh; she shall be called Woman, because she
> was taken out of Man." For this cause a man shall leave his
> father and mother, and shall cleave to his wife; and they
> shall become one flesh.
>
> —GENESIS 2:23–24

Man and woman were designed by God from the beginning to be distinctly individual, free to make choices, yet created to be vitally one with each other.

> He created *them* male and female, and He blessed *them*,
> and named *them Man* in the day when they were created.
>
> —GENESIS 5:2, *emphasis added*

Each person, whether male *or* female, was created in the image of God, male *and* female, with both male and female attributes. I have no problem whatsoever calling God "Father" and relating to Him as such. My childhood experiences with my earthly father built into me positive attitudes and comfortable feelings toward men. "Father" to me means a special quality of strength, power, protection, logic, and authority. I also experienced tenderness and gentleness flowing from the heart of my father.

Because of that good foundation built in me, I can easily see those qualities flowing in perfection from the heart of my heavenly Father. What we have experienced or judged our fathers to be always colors to some extent our pictures of God, the great authority figure. If I had been neglected or abused by my father and had with futility longed for him to be what I needed him to be...or if I had learned to identify my mother as *the only* one who could understand and comfort...I would probably be among the ranks of those today who lobby for inclusive language in the Bible (using generic pronouns instead of masculine ones for deity).

Man is designed to experience and act primarily out of the masculine role of his being and to yearn for the woman to meet him. In their one-fleshness she will express that part of him that he cannot. Woman is designed to experience and act primarily from a uniquely feminine base, though she has masculine qualities within her. Her husband is to unite with her in such a way as to fulfill and express easily that masculine part of her that she cannot.

My parents weren't perfect, but they represented to me an unusually healthy balance of a gentle, strong, *masculine* father *united* with a tender, strong, *feminine* mother. He was the head of the house, though profoundly influenced by her. When he was gone from home as a traveling salesman, she managed very capably under varieties of stress, and he was a powerful balm to settle her emotions the moment he came through the door.

I called him *Father*, but I never thought of him apart from my mother. They were a unit. For that reason I have no difficulty understanding how God could create man and woman and call *them* Man. When the Bible says: "he"—"him"—"his," I know that means me and mine as well. And when I call God "Father," I never think of Him apart from gentleness and tenderness.

## HEALING FOR A NEGATIVE OR FRACTURED FATHER-IMAGE

If you were terribly wounded by your father (or another authority figure) and now find blockages in relation to Father God, the beginning of freedom is to choose to forgive your earthly father. Forgiveness does not excuse his transgressions or his abdication of authority and affectionate nurture. He will stand accountable before God.

On the other hand, forgiveness of another person has little to do with the actual guilt of the person who is being forgiven. The supposed offender may be innocent. Or he may be guilty of even more than the wounded person is aware. To choose to forgive is to say, "I am angry. I have held resentment and bitterness in my heart against my father (or whoever it is). I recognize that this is poison inside of me that will prevent or destroy my life, as well as the lives of others. It colors my perceptions and can pollute every relationship I try to develop. I want to be rid of it so that I may bless others and be free to trust God."

When you choose, in prayer, to forgive, the Lord takes that choice and makes it real. It may be necessary to repeat the choice again and again. After all, powerful resentments were built by a series of choices in reaction to pain that may have spanned years. You may even be afraid to let anger or resentment go, because it has seemed to be your only defense. Without it, you fear being overcome by the one who would violate you again.

If you have already tried over and over in your own strength to forgive and now come to prayer with the realization that you are helpless to accomplish it alone, you may experience a miracle of release—because your heart is ripe. The Lord will let you struggle as much as necessary in the process of choosing in order to write the necessity of your intention and other lessons indelibly upon your heart. But He will be faithful to accomplish this goal, because it is His will to heal and set free.

When the poison of unforgiveness is finally gone from your heart, then will you be able to receive the fullness and comfort of healing and affirmation from Father God. You will have eyes to see and ears to hear. And the kindness of His healing will lead you to the blessing of repentance for your own sinful reactions. When you have known the love and kindness of God, you no longer fear acknowledging and taking responsibility for your own sin. You no longer fear vulnerability in relationships. God will build something gloriously new and beautiful on the foundation of forgiveness and repentance.

## MEN AND WOMEN COMPLETE ONE ANOTHER

In one sense, my husband is that other part of me without which I am not *complete.* And I am that other part of him. "One flesh" refers to far more than physical union. It is a meeting and uniting of two people in body, mind, and spirit.

God's plan for our coming together is *not* one-half plus one-half equals *one whole.* The formula for our union is more accurately described as one plus one equals one—greater, deeper, and richer than either of us could be alone; it's more like the impossible math of one times one equals one hundred.

It is very important to understand that though we are to complete one another in the one-flesh relationship of marriage, a man or woman who never marries is not thereby prevented from becoming whole. Every person's *wholeness* depends upon a developed personal relationship with the Lord Jesus Christ. He is our righteousness and our balance; He gives us our identity and enables us to experience unity.

> For all of you who were baptized into Christ have clothed yourselves with Christ. There is neither Jew nor Greek, there is neither slave nor free man, there is neither male nor female; for you are all one in Christ Jesus.
> —GALATIANS 3:27–28

Ideally our corporate wholeness is to be blessedly completed when all that we are is given into the one-flesh marriage relationship that God has designed. Unfortunately, since sin entered the picture early in the history of mankind, all of us contribute significantly less than individual wholeness to the union.

But the Lord's plan is not defeated. He is able to use our deepest fractures and roughest exteriors powerfully and effectively in His redemptive process when we invite Him to do so. We are blessedly designed to be like abrasives to each other until the Lord in us has accomplished His plan—the polishing of a corporate jewel.

## The Beginning of the Battle

The age-old "battle of the sexes" began when *both* woman and man sinned and lied to God about it.

| Woman | Man |
|---|---|
| 1. Talked to the serpent. | 1. Failed to protect Eve. |
| 2. Failing in discernment, believed the serpent and ate of the forbidden fruit, desiring to be like God. (He would have matured her and taught her in His wisdom and timing. She took her life into her own hands.) | 2. Failed to communicate clearly which tree was for eating and which was not. (Eve was not yet made when the commandments were given.) |
| 3. Seduced her husband to eat with her. | 3. Chose to follow his wife rather than the commandments of God. (This is idolatry.) |

If *either* of them had been eating adequately of the tree of life in the middle of the Garden of Eden, they would not have been so vulnerable to sin. They would not have failed.

## The Merciful Love of God Rejected

Neither took responsibility for her or his own transgression, though God gave each of them ample opportunity to do so. The third chapter of Genesis relates the grandest case of buck-passing in all of history:

> And they heard the sound of the LORD God walking in the garden in the cool of the day, and the man and his wife hid

> themselves from the presence of the LORD God among the trees of the garden. Then the LORD God called to the man, and said to him, "Where are you?" And he said, "I heard the sound of Thee in the garden, and *I was afraid because I was naked; so I hid myself.*"
>
> —GENESIS 3:8–10, *emphasis added*

The Lord knew exactly where Adam was and why. His question gave Adam an opportunity to confess, but instead he lied. The guilty couple had always known they were naked (Gen. 2:25). They were now ashamed and afraid because they had sinned. They had become defiled by Satan and were perceiving everything through his eyes. Therefore they could no longer trust the nature of God.

> And He said, "*Who told you that you were naked? Have you eaten from the tree of which I commanded you not to eat?*" And the man said, "The *woman* whom *Thou* gavest to be with me, *she* gave me from the tree, and I ate." Then the LORD God said to the woman, "*What is this you have done?*" And the woman said, "The *serpent* deceived me, and I ate."
>
> —GENESIS 3:11–13, *emphasis added*

Because of sin for which neither of them was repentant, Adam and Eve lost their relationship with God and the quality of life with which God had originally blessed them. Eve's desire had always been for her husband; now it would be an inordinate desire. Because of her fractured trust in God and an unholy fear of Him, she would look for and demand from her husband what only God can give. The pain of bringing forth children would be greatly multiplied (Gen. 3:16). She could no longer rest in God, and stress would always multiply pain.

Adam had always ruled over his wife, but now, because of sin, his rule would be possessive, dominating, and controlling. Still today there are many religious men who, in their fear, confusion, and unhealed childhood wounds, make a perverted use of the Bible to excuse and perpetuate domination and control over women. The turning point of nearly every religious movement that has gone into heresy and cultism has been marked by legalism and the subjugation of women.

Marriages have collapsed when husbands have tried to force their wives to be what they wanted, rather than meeting them where they are and loving and nurturing them to freely become what God wanted. Husbands were disappointed and disillusioned with what they had "made" because the wives were no longer the adequate helpmeets God had given them, and they didn't have the discernment to see what had gone wrong. Many women, eager to please but insecure about their own identities and worth, have allowed and even invited men to treat them so.

Man's and woman's relationship with God was fractured, and their relationship with the earth was now characterized by toil and sweat.

> For the creation (nature) was subjected to frailty (to futility, condemned to frustration), not because of some intentional fault on its part, but by the will of Him Who so subjected it—[yet] with the hope that nature (creation) itself will be set free from its bondage to decay and corruption [and gain an entrance] into the glorious freedom of God's children.
> —Romans 8:20–21, AMP

God knew that mankind was now subject to the curse of a fallen nature, which would ultimately bring destruction upon themselves and creation. However, God never intended to leave us that way. His love for us is so great that He has made propitiation through Jesus Christ, restoring us to the glory we experienced in the beginning.

> *For I consider that the sufferings of this present time are not worthy to be compared with the glory that is to be revealed to us.* For the anxious longing of the creation waits eagerly for the revealing of the sons of God. For the creation was subjected to futility, not of its own will, but because of Him who subjected it, in hope that the *creation itself also will be set free from its slavery to corruption into the freedom of the glory of the children of God.* For we know that the whole creation groans and suffers the pains of childbirth together until now. And not only this, but also we ourselves, having the first fruits of the Spirit, even we ourselves groan within ourselves, waiting eagerly for our adoption as sons, the redemption of our body. *For in hope we have been saved,* but hope that is seen is not hope; for why does one also hope for what he sees? But if we hope for what we do not see, *with perseverance we wait eagerly for it.*
>
> And in the same way the Spirit also helps our weakness; for we do not know how to pray as we should, but the *Spirit Himself intercedes for us with groanings too deep for words*; and He who searches the hearts knows what the mind of the Spirit is, because *He intercedes for the saints according to the will of God. And we know that God causes all things to work together for good to those who love God, to those who are called according to His purpose.*
> —ROMANS 8:18–28, *emphasis added*

Thank God He made a way to restore our broken relationship with Him. Jesus *is* the Way. Sin separated us from God, but now we can experience complete fellowship with Him through His Son.

However painful your present situation may be, know that "God causes all things to work together for good to those who love God." Think about it: what is the probability that you would read this book if everything were going smoothly? I would say that it is highly unlikely. But the fact that you realize your need for God's help is the beginning of allowing Him to cause "all things to work together for your good."

Your acknowledgment of needing His help to restore your relationship with Him and with your spouse allows Him to move on your behalf. And when words seem superfluous, allow the Holy Spirit to guide you.

## GOD'S OLD TESTAMENT PURPOSE AND MODEL FOR WOMEN

In Proverbs 31:11–31, a woman is valued and called to be all she can be. We read that an excellent wife is worth far more than jewels. Her husband's heart trusts in her, and he will have no lack of gain. She does him good all the days of her life.

She is industrious, healthy, strong in body, self-confident, ministering to others, and well dressed.

She affirms her husband, and because of that, he has prestige.

She works in the business world, is unafraid, is well ordered, is consistent, and conducts herself with dignity and kindness.

She is not an extension of her husband. She is rewarded, blessed by her husband and children.

Scripture says:

Her children rise up and bless her; her husband also, and he praises her.... Give her the product of her hands, and let her works praise her in the gates.

—PROVERBS 31:28, 31

Rachel D. Levine, while writing her doctoral thesis on women's roles in Judaism during the early centuries, wrote that the Proverbs 31 passage has been held up for hundreds of years as the ideal to which Jewish women should aspire:

> What did the woman do, and what were her responsibilities? Within the home, she had total authority to see that all domestic duties were performed, and in addition to her own labors, supervised the work of the servants. She made sure that ample supplies of both food and clothing were available for all household members. What was not locally attainable she imported from other areas as necessary. In addition to providing for her dependents, she was in charge of the "cottage industry" of her home and dealt with the local merchants in selling them the goods thus produced. She was active in real estate ventures, and supervised the agricultural workers. She ensured the family's survival during hard times by a savings program, and was the prime educator of her children.
>
> In addition to her domestic and commercial ventures, she was active in local charity work. Her religious duties were not neglected, and she was known for her piety and devotion to the Lord. As a result, her husband was free to concentrate on his endeavors without worrying about his household affairs, secure in the knowledge that all was being done properly without the need for his constant supervision.[1]

What a contrast this is to the attitude of some men today who mistakenly have thought that the Bible gives them the mandate to tell their wives what to wear, cook, think, say, and where to go, what to do, and how to do it.

When one partner so dominates the other, he cancels out the other part of his own flesh. My husband, John, tells people that if I should ever shut my mouth, he would lose half his wisdom. Then he hastens to add with an affectionate chuckle, "But I don't think there is a chance of that ever happening!"

In the New Testament, the woman is called to give all she can be and to shine.

> No one, after lighting a lamp, puts it away in a cellar, nor under a peck-measure, but on the lampstand, in order that those who enter may see the light.
>
> —LUKE 11:33

In biblical culture, the head is the place of honor. Feet are considered to be the lowest, least-honored part of the body. If the Bible meant for us to dishonor or diminish woman, or give anyone license to walk on her, she would have been called "an old shoe," not a "crown."

> An excellent wife is the crown of her husband.
>
> —PROVERBS 12:4

The Bible sets forth the ideal, and much of the Law is written to protect the woman from violation. However, the sin nature being what it is, women have been oppressed in many cultures throughout history. Still, wherever Jesus Christ has not been made Lord of men's hearts, subjugation and persecution of women persist.

## GOD'S ORIGINAL PLAN FOR MALE/FEMALE RELATIONSHIPS IS TO BE RESTORED IN CHRIST

Jesus Christ came to bring recovery of sight to the blind and good news to the afflicted, to bind up the brokenhearted, to proclaim liberty to captives and freedom to prisoners, and to set free those who are downtrodden (Isa. 61:1–3; Luke 4:18). Jesus befriended women, received ministry from them, and defended, honored, and respected them. He set an example for all to follow.

Saint Paul has unfairly received some bad press from many who, in their ignorance of the culture of biblical times, believe he thought poorly of women. In actuality, he followed Jesus as one of the greatest liberationists of all time. He took care to acknowledge with gratitude those women who had helped significantly in the work of the church: Priscilla, Claudia, Phoebe, Mary, Tryphaena, Tryphosa, Rufus's mother, Julia, Nereus's sister, Apphia, and others. In Philippians 4:3 he writes, "Indeed, true comrade, I ask you also to help these women who have shared my struggle in the cause of the gospel."

Let us take a closer look at some often-quoted and frequently misunderstood passages from Paul's letters. In Ephesians 5, Paul taught that mutual submission was to be coupled with sacrificial love and respect:

> And be subject to one another in the fear of Christ. Wives, be subject to your own husbands, as to the Lord. For the husband is head of the wife, as Christ also is the head of the church, He Himself being Savior of the body. But as the church is subject to Christ, so also the wives ought to be to their husbands in everything.
>
> —EPHESIANS 5:21–24

Notice first that "be subject to one another" is said in the context of marital relationships. No one had ever before told a man to be subject to a woman, yet here Saint Paul clearly says to be subject to *one another*! Notice that he carefully says first to be subject to one another before he goes on to describe the husband's position as head of the wife.

Notice the word *as* in the Scripture quote. Paul is presenting a clear model for headship and submission. *How* is Christ head of the church? By laying down His life for her sake, that she might have life. And by inviting her to accept that gift— never robbing her of her free will. Never forcing her. Never condemning. Never shutting her out. Loving her unconditionally. Strengthening her so she can stand. Protecting her.

*How* is the church subject to Christ? By voluntarily offering all that she is, with commitment to love unconditionally and to serve with sensitivity, faithfulness, honor, and respect.

> Husbands, love your wives, just as Christ also loved the church and gave Himself up for her; that He might sanctify her....Husbands ought also to love their own wives as their own bodies. He who loves his own wife loves himself; for no one ever hated his own flesh, but nourishes and cherishes it, just as Christ also does the church, because we are members of His body.
>
> —EPHESIANS 5:25–26, 28–30

We read here a clear call to *give*, not to *get*. The command is to minister to the other for the other's sake, not self-centeredly demanding for our own sake, and especially not a husband demanding and controlling because of his so-called superior position. Notice the emphasis on the one-flesh nature of husband and wife and the relationship between loving, nurturing, and cherishing.

Love is not merely a romantic feeling. It is a *choice* to nurture and cherish unconditionally so that the spouse might grow in sanctification into the most he/she can be.

It is at the times when I least deserve my husband's cherishing that I most need his love, and certainly his nurture. More than once I have said to John, "I'm upset. I'm a mess. I don't want or need your analysis, your advice, or your rebuke right now. I just need you to hug me!" And when he puts his bewilderment aside to wrap those strong arms around his undeserving wife, I am strengthened to receive all the other things he'd like to present to me. He needs that same consideration from me.

> Let the wife see to it that she respect her husband.
> —EPHESIANS 5:33

It is difficult for many women to respect their husbands because they can easily make long lists of their transgressions and failings. But respect is something much more than approval of performance. I am called to "see to it" that I respect my husband's position—not to mother, lacerate, or emasculate him.

I am called to respect him as a person, not only for his admirable qualities, but also as one who has problems, feelings, and sensitivities that need to be met according to the nature of Christ in me. It is to our benefit if I respect the fact that his experiences and approach to many situations are often different from mine and that I am not always comprehensive or right in my perceptions and understandings.

To respect another is not the same as to agree with him. Respect does not prevent appropriate confrontation. Rather, respect calls us to discipline our hearts to maintain attitudes that will affirm the other in every way possible—and to discipline our actions and words to edify, not to undermine or annihilate the other.

In Ephesians 4:15–32, Paul emphasized the importance of *corporateness* in Christian faith and life, and he gave directions for growing in it:

- ∾ Lay aside the old self (v. 22).

- ∾ Be renewed in the spirit of your mind (v. 23).

- ∾ Put on the new self (v. 24).

- ∾ Lay aside falsehood (v. 25).

- ∾ Be angry, but sin not (v. 26).

- ∾ Do not give the devil an opportunity (v. 27).

- ∾ Let no unwholesome word proceed from your mouth (v. 29).

- ∾ Let all bitterness, wrath, anger, clamor, and slander be put away from you, and all malice (v. 31).

- ∾ Be kind to one another, tenderhearted, *forgiving each other*, just as God in Christ also has forgiven you (v. 32, emphasis added).

## CLEARING UP MISCONCEPTIONS ABOUT PAUL'S INSTRUCTIONS

Oftentimes people, especially church leadership, will quote Paul's instructions about women exercising authority over men in an effort to prove their point that women should not be in leadership over men. But it is time to set the record straight about that misconception.

> Let a woman quietly receive instructions with entire submissiveness. But I do not allow a woman to teach or exercise authority ["*usurp authority*" in KJV] over a man, but to remain quiet.
> —1 TIMOTHY 2:11–12

Years ago John and I were invited to speak for an ecumenical gathering at a restaurant in St. Louis. The meeting proceeded quietly and smoothly until I stepped up to the microphone. A rather large, red-faced man instantly jumped to his feet and loudly challenged my right to teach. Quickly, Paul Haglin (the pastor in charge of the meeting), along with my husband, stepped in front of me, and Paul declared with gentle but firm authority that since he had invited me to speak, there was no way in which I could possibly be usurping authority.

The man refused to hear, and his voice rose as he raged on. John said, "It is clear this man has no intention to hear and intends only to disrupt. Get him out of here." Several men from the host church physically picked him up and carried him outside.

I continued to teach, overwhelmingly grateful that I had been defended by strong, masculine partners in the gospel. I realized also that the experience had brought healing to a place deep inside of me that had still felt unprotected because my father had traveled away from home so much when I was a child. I had prayed about it. This experience confirmed my prayer and strengthened my faith that my heavenly Father is ever present and ready to take the initiative on my behalf.

Later we learned that this was not that man's first time to be forcefully transported to outer courts; he had usurped authority many times in many places as he set himself up as a self-appointed prophetic "authority" on the Word. He finally "authoritated" his way into a psychiatric ward.

### *Scripture needs to be read in the context in which it was written.*

First Timothy 2:11 was written in the context of the usurping of authority. Also, Paul was well aware that Christians were already upsetting the world (Acts 17:6). He had the wisdom to make it known that he was neither teaching nor modeling extremes that would suddenly and unnecessarily upset established order in the churches. People then, as now, did not accept change with gracious ease.

As a case in point, John and I served in a church in Illinois early in our ministry. Someone gave the church a beautiful new altar. Our logic said that the old altar had served well for an untold number of years. Though it bore the scars of much use, it could serve in another capacity for a long time as well. But the new altar was much more appropriate to the décor of a newly redecorated chancel.

With respect and honor, we moved the old altar to the first floor where the young people could appreciate it in their chapel area, and we installed the new one in the main sanctuary. Immediately dissensions crescendoed into accusations and insults! One would have thought that we had moved God.

Paul had also a practical purpose in mind when he said that women should be quiet. First Corinthians 14 sets out a reasonable order for considerate participation and sharing in the churches, spelling it out clearly to everyone concerning when it is appropriate for one to speak and another to keep silent.

> And the spirits of prophets are subject to prophets; for
> *God is not a God of confusion but of peace,* as in all the
> churches of the saints.
>
> —1 CORINTHIANS 14:32, *emphasis added*

The following passage, then, needs to be read in the context of
the rest of the chapter, within Paul's concern to preserve order.

> Let the women keep silent in the churches; for they
> are not permitted to speak, but let them subject them-
> selves, just as the Law also says. And if they desire to learn
> anything, let them ask their own husbands at home; for it
> is improper for a woman to speak in church. Was it from
> you that the word of God *first* went forth? Or has it come
> to you *only*? If anyone thinks he is a prophet or spiritual,
> let him recognize that the things which I write to you are
> the Lord's commandment.
>
> —1 CORINTHIANS 14:34–37, *emphasis added*

There is certainly no sexist language here:

> Until *we all* attain to the unity of the faith, and of the knowl-
> edge of the Son of God, to a mature man, to the measure of
> the stature which belongs to the fullness of Christ.
>
> —EPHESIANS 4:13, *emphasis added*

> …speaking the truth in love, *we* are to grow up in all
> aspects into Him, who is the head, even Christ.
>
> —EPHESIANS 4:15, *emphasis added*

To understand what is going on here, we need to divest our
minds of the pictures we have of our own home groups with
everyone, male and female, seated together in comfortable
circles in someone's living room. Scripture must be read in the
context of the culture of the East. (That culture remains the

same in many aspects throughout the Middle and Far East.) Traditionally, men and women were not seated together in the temple worship. Men gathered in the main room; women were seated behind a partition. When people met in homes, even for social gatherings, the men and women were normally separated.

In the late 1950s John and I were privileged to have a beautiful couple from India, Russell and Vickie Chandran, visit in our home on several occasions. They were Christians doing graduate study for a year at Chicago Theological Seminary, which was then part of the University of Chicago. He was the president of a theological seminary in Bangalore, and she was a schoolteacher. We very much enjoyed our fellowship with them.

As the time approached for them to return to their homeland, Vickie said that she would have to be very careful at home for a time. She had grown accustomed in America to visiting and sharing openly in mixed company. It had been a delight to her and had become comfortably a part of her.

She was afraid that when she returned home she might forget that such an interchange was not allowed. She might offend someone, thereby disgracing her husband. They were bound by their culture to act in ways neither still believed to be appropriate. We had witnessed the deep love and respect Russell had for his wife. In Christ, he valued her person and her opinion, and he welcomed her expression of who she was.

Can you put yourself in the position of a woman in the early church? For centuries there had been much oppression of women everywhere in the Eastern world. Despite the ideal set forth in Judaism and described in Proverbs 31, there were still many restrictions upon women, particularly in the area of speaking to or participating with men in public and in the areas of religious service. A woman could be divorced by her husband by his simply setting her belongings on the doorstep, thereby disgracing her and her entire family.

This is the principal reason for the New Testament teachings concerning divorce—protection of women—that they not be put out as if they were chattel! Jesus had talked with, respected, defended, and honored women. He came offering a new quality of life to everyone, far beyond their wildest dreams. They had witnessed or heard of miracles that boggled their minds. Today we are so familiar with the teachings of Jesus and take for granted the freedoms that Christianity has won for us, and so we may miss the excitement that was enjoyed in the early church. Early Christians were on fire! So on fire, in fact, that they were willing to risk their lives.

Christian women had such an excitement building in them they could hardly contain themselves! Imagine yourself in an early church meeting. Earthshaking things are being talked about in the main room—lifesaving matters the Lord has intended for you also. You desperately don't want to miss a word, but you can't hear clearly all that is being said because you are set off to the side with the other women behind some sort of partition (usually a cloth curtain or tapestry). You miss something, and before you can stop to think, you are trying to get your neighbor's attention to find out what it was. Perhaps you are whispering across the curtain to your husband, if he is close by, "Ben, what did he say?" And by so doing, you cause a disturbance.

It is no wonder Paul told the women that if they desired to learn something, they should ask their husbands at home (1 Cor. 14:35). Paul goes on to properly reprimand the women for their lack of propriety: "Or came it [the Word of God] unto you only?" (v. 36, KJV). Their undisciplined excitement had caused them to be self-centeredly inconsiderate of others. But this directive is only part of a chapter that is an appeal for order-liness, self-discipline, and consideration of everyone, one for the other, that the whole body might be edified: "Let all things be done properly and in orderly manner" (1 Cor. 14:40).

### *Women, according to Scripture, were not excluded from prophesying.*

Women have long held an important role in the Scriptures, and two examples in particular come to mind. One example is the evangelist Philip's four virgin daughters.

> Now this man [Philip the evangelist] had four virgin daughters who were prophetesses.
>
> —ACTS 21:9

What little we do know about Philip's four virgin daughters is that they were active in public speaking and prophesying, so much so that they are recorded in biblical history.

Anna, a prophetess who was active well into her retirement years, is yet another example.

> And there was a prophetess, Anna the daughter of Phanuel, of the tribe of Asher. She was advanced in years, having lived with a husband seven years after her marriage, and then as a widow to the age of eighty-four. And she never left the temple, serving night and day with fastings and prayers. *And at that very moment she came up and began giving thanks to God, and continued to speak of Him to all those who were looking for the redemption of Jerusalem.*
>
> —LUKE 2:36–38, *emphasis added*

"That very moment" was the moment when Simeon blessed Jesus and His parents at the time of His circumcision, amazing them with the declaration that this child would be "a light of revelation to the Gentiles, and the glory of Thy people Israel" (Luke 2:32).

### Women were not excluded from instructing.

> Now a certain Jew named Apollos, an Alexandrian by birth, an eloquent man, came to Ephesus; and he was mighty in the Scriptures. This man had been instructed in the way of the Lord; and being fervent in spirit, he was speaking and teaching accurately the things concerning Jesus, being acquainted only with the baptism of John; and he began to speak out boldly in the synagogue. But when Priscilla and Aquila heard him, *they* took him aside and explained to him the way of God more accurately.
> —ACTS 18:24–26, *emphasis added*

Observe that Paul is clearly saying that Priscilla taught a man more accurately concerning the Word. Notice also that Priscilla is mentioned first. In the protocol of the Bible, this means that Priscilla was a leader in their ministry as a team.

Paul's impartiality toward the role of women in ministry is solidified in subsequent scriptures. He goes on to establish the need for mutual dependence between men and woman in working in the kingdom.

1. Paul speaks of *mutual* authority in husband/wife relationships.

> The wife does not have authority over her own body, but the husband does; and likewise also the husband does not have authority over his own body, but the wife does.
> —1 CORINTHIANS 7:4

## 2. Paul also speaks of *mutual* sanctification.

For the unbelieving husband is sanctified through his wife, and the unbelieving wife is sanctified through her believing husband; for otherwise your children are unclean, but now they are holy.

—1 CORINTHIANS 7:14

## 3. And he speaks of *corporate* belonging.

We are members of His body.

—EPHESIANS 5:30

For this cause a man shall leave his father and mother, and shall cleave to his wife; and the two shall become one flesh.

—EPHESIANS 5:31; CF. GENESIS 2:24

*You are fellow citizens with the saints, and are of God's household,* having been built upon the foundation of the apostles and prophets, Christ Jesus Himself being the corner stone, in whom the *whole* building, being fitted *together* is growing into a holy temple in the Lord; in whom you also are being built *together* into a dwelling of God in the Spirit.

—EPHESIANS 2:19–22, *emphasis added*

This is God's perfect plan for all of us, that *together* we may truly become the church through whom the manifold wisdom of God will be made known even to the rulers and authorities in the heavenly places (Eph. 3:10).

For us to participate in what God will accomplish, our petty "pecking orders" must die, along with our anxious scrambling for recognition and position. Our needs to control our lives and the lives of others and to defend or exalt ourselves at the expense of others must die. Male and female, we must find our identity, worth, and purpose first in the Lord Jesus.

There are no second-class citizens in the kingdom of God. You are a fellow citizen in His household. Let Him heal your wounds, forgive your sins, dispel your fears, sort out your confusions, and reveal to you the glory that you are in Him. Once that reality has been established in your heart, no one will be able to take it from you.

*Chapter 3*

# LEARNING *to* LIVE
# WITH FEELINGS

E VERYBODY HAS FEELINGS. SOMETIMES they are our blessings, sometimes afflictions.

Some feelings are like embracing currents of light, fresh air that lifts and carries us to joyful and exciting heights. Others are oppressive mountains of heaviness, pressing and flattening even our innermost parts to the point of despair until pain gives way to numbness.

We have the capacity to feel wonderfully full to the point of explosion—full of gratitude, bursting with love, eight and a half months pregnant with expectation, overwhelmed with indescribable *wows*! Or we can feel so overcome with anger and frustration that the least stimulus is enough to blow the lid off our accumulated steam.

Common feelings find varieties of expression, which are often not understood.

## TEARS

Tears are a natural and healthy emotional release.

All of us, male and female, have experienced some degree of hurt, anger, disappointment, grief, and sorrow. Perhaps unhealed pain has multiplied within you, and your capacity to contain it has been strained to the breaking point. You have felt uncomfortably pressured from within and disoriented. Finally, tears have leaked uncontrollably through cracks in your fleshly armor. And you have been embarrassed, fearful of being out of control, feeling guilty for seeming not to be "strong," not recognizing that God has created a safety valve in you and a blessed healing release through your tears.

Perhaps a loved one unwittingly has put you down by pressuring you to "pull yourself together." Or someone with misguided zeal may have knocked you into an emotional hole with heavy exhortations to "cheer up" or "have faith," when your weeping had nothing to do with a lack of faith, nor was it yet time to rejoice. You have felt misunderstood, condemned, angry, and disgruntled with people in general and with yourself for your responses. Miserable, you have wrapped the darkness around you, not even wanting to come out. Hiding seemed to offer more comfort than being hit again.

### Jesus wept.

Even Jesus, who was God incarnate, showed that tears are a normal part of everyday living. Jesus was "deeply moved in spirit, and...troubled" (John 11:33) as He identified with those whom He found weeping over Lazarus's death, and He Himself wept (v. 35). He did not rush in, announcing He was going to raise Lazarus from the dead. Nor did He reprove the people for their tears. He entered into their sorrow and participated with them before He performed the miracle of resurrection He had planned beforehand.

> Blessed be the God and Father of our Lord Jesus Christ, the Father of mercies and God of all comfort; who comforts us in all our affliction so that we may be able to comfort those who are in any affliction with the comfort with which we ourselves are comforted by God....Our comfort is abundant through Christ.
>
> —2 CORINTHIANS 1:3–5

He still bears our grief and carries our sorrows (Isa. 53:4) as He comforts us and calls us to do as He has done.

### Let the tears flow.

Tears are not a sign of weakness. I encourage you to let the tears flow when you have something to cry about, and not to believe anyone who tells you that grief and sorrow are a sign of lack of faith or a work of the devil. The ability to cry is a gift from God. When you receive that gift and allow it to work in you appropriately, then you are much less likely to suffer from the physical and emotional side effects of repression, such as high blood pressure, ulcers, nervous breakdowns, or depression. If you are suppressing and trying to control your emotions to put forward a courageous front, then you are hurting yourself most of all.

Most women seem to be able to cry more easily than most men. I don't believe crying has anything at all to do with weakness. It has a great deal to do with permission given by our culture from the time we were children. As little girls, we didn't receive the repeated messages that little boys did: "Don't be a crybaby." "Sissies cry." "When are you going to act like a man?"

*Suppressed tears may come up in twisted, embarrassing, and even hurtful guise.*

Most men have tender emotions, though many try to deny it. Men need to learn that not only is it OK to cry, but it is also very healthy to express themselves with tears.

John is proud of his Native American ancestry and vividly remembers his mother telling him, "Osage Indian boys don't cry." That message was strongly reinforced by strains of stoicism and reserve inherited through English streams in his family.

Added to these influences was the presence of strong defensive walls he had built to keep from being vulnerable to criticism and ridicule. Therefore, the phrase "don't cry" so powerfully influenced his sense of who he was, and was so integrally structured into his automatic response system, that it created problems, especially for me.

John is gifted with an extremely sensitive spirit. He could easily tune in to the upsets and hurts of others. But if he felt any inclination to weep for them or with them, his internal programming automatically set him to respond defensively in one or both of two modes—turn off or laugh. It didn't bother me when he would laugh at a tearjerker movie. Strangers sitting nearby often thought he was weird for laughing during tearful scenes, but it didn't matter because the probability that we would ever see them again was highly unlikely.

On one occasion, however, I was embarrassed, and anxious, when John laughed at a man who took an awkward fall over his dog's leash in the park. Granted, it was a comical sight, but that man could have been hurt, and that was also a part of John's perception—hence his need to vent his emotions in his unusual way. The man was so angry at John's outward reaction that he actually started toward him to punch him and was stopped only by a sincere and profuse apology from my husband.

The real problems were much deeper. Sometimes I needed to spill out my hurt and frustration by crying. In those moments I was not seeking advice or counsel from anyone, especially not my husband. All I wanted was a warm, strong shoulder to cry on—someone to accept me and meet me in my mess and love me to balance again. It was crushing to receive his "turn off" or "laugh" messages.

I would plead with him, "John, listen to me. I don't want you to be my counselor. I just want you to hold me!" "John, it's not funny!"

"I'm not laughing at you," he would say.

"Then why is your face looking like that?" I replied.

By then (the conversation being somewhat condensed here) the prickles of budding anger were beginning to emerge from within me, and I had given him an excuse for not coming near. For years I stewed in the heat of periodic angers, and he cooled in the isolation of his cave, until together we discovered the roots in both of us that created the dynamic and began to learn to confront and overcome the "enemy" in a joint effort.

### *Sometimes we cry the tears another can't cry.*

Another problem issuing from the "don't cry" syndrome is that sometimes a person cries through the tears of another. In other words, a person's emotions are so bottled up that the only way she experiences release from her emotions is to make (or see) another person cry.

Early in our marriage John would assume such a load of people's emotions as he ministered in the parish that he couldn't release those emotions fast enough. Without realizing what he was doing, he would come home and pick on me until I cried. It was foundationally and securely built into John that a real man would not for any reason strike a woman, so he never even came close to abusing me physically. Nor has he even raised his voice more than once or twice. He was, rather, in our early years together, an expert on "home refrigeration" or the "soft put-down."

Wives live within the kind of one-flesh relationship in which, choose it or not, we really do bear our husbands' burdens (Gal. 6:2).

> Rejoice with those who rejoice, and weep with those who weep.
>
> —ROMANS 12:15

By the same token, husbands can experience emotional release through their wives. As my tears flowed, John would feel relieved. Then he would struggle with guilt for feeling good when I was so miserable. When he finally experienced enough healing and strength of spirit to do his own crying, it was marvelous to experience the calm river of peace that carried us both.

### Sometimes a spouse's desire to protect can do more harm than good.

Often a husband won't share his problems because he believes he is protecting his wife. The reality of such "protection" is that it only afflicts her. He doesn't realize that his wife will feel the heaviness or upset that emanates from within him and will bear his unidentified burdens more stressfully. She may bear his burdens so often that she will frequently be saddened and may cry so easily and unexplainably that he thinks he has married someone emotionally immature or unstable.

Many wives have carried such weights for so long that it

has seriously affected their health. Perhaps your husband can't share with you the details of a problem he is working on without breaking a valid responsibility regarding government or job security or confidentiality. But if he will learn to acknowledge generally the presence of a problem and invite you to pray with him for wisdom and confidence, protection and refreshment, he will bless you and lighten the load you carry for him.

***Inability or refusal to deal appropriately with our emotions can result in violence toward those we love.***

Over the years we counseled numerous cases of wife-beating in which the husband was horrified at what he had inflicted on the woman he dearly loved. "I don't know what came over me" was the response we often heard.

In each case we explored his relationship with his mother and other primary female figures in his childhood to determine what long-suppressed hurts, angers, and frustrations he might now be unconsciously projecting onto his wife. Often this was a significant factor. He had suffered some sort of mental, emotional, or physical abuse as a child. Overt reaction had only brought more abuse, so he had developed habitual ways of avoiding conflict and of suppressing his feelings until often they were hidden—even from himself.

Sometimes we found no history of abuse, but rather a family upbringing in which emotional issues were never discussed and thus never resolved. As a sensitive boy, one counselee had absorbed quantities of unexpressed and unidentified energies. He couldn't distinguish his own feelings from what he sensed from deep levels in others; he didn't even know it was possible to empathize involuntarily with others. But those undercurrent emotions had accumulated in his heart until he was like a land mine waiting to be stepped on.

Years later a conflict developed at work. Because it seemed insignificant at the time, and because he had never developed skills of recognizing, acknowledging, and disciplining his own feelings, he characteristically ignored or suppressed them. He didn't know he was already fueled to the limit with combustible material. Then he came home to his wife who "stepped" on him with an innocent reminder to carry out the trash. *Pow!* The emotional land mine exploded at last.

Sometimes an abusive husband is simply one who has swallowed the lie that a *strong* man *must* handle his own problems. He has struggled to do this for so long that finally the load is so overpoweringly heavy that it overcomes him. He drops it for fear that it will crush him, and he lashes out, blindly objectifying his desperation and anger on his wife, children, the dog, or any other person or object near at hand.

If you have been the recipient of abusive behavior, please consider this:

1. *You did not do anything to cause your husband to beat you.* It may be true that you have made judgments on men that they will act that way because you grew up in an abusive situation. You may still have some forgiving to do. Your expectations and your behavior may need some radical changing. But your husband must take *full* responsibility for his own sinful actions and reactions. He made choices, consciously or unconsciously, for which he is accountable. You are called to deal only with *your* sin.

2. *You cannot save or change your husband.* That is not your job. Only Jesus Himself is big enough

to transform lives. The goodness of your love may threaten him because it makes him feel vulnerable, and vulnerability can be a fearful thing. The sweetness of your love alone, and the more it melts his heart, may force him to isolate himself or do something mean to cause you to back off. The power and wisdom of Jesus' love can eventually give him strength of spirit to admit his need and seek help.

Pray that the eyes of his heart be enlightened (Eph. 1:18) and that he be strengthened in his spirit (Eph. 3:16), and continue to love him as best you can. But don't delude yourself into thinking that if you just love him enough he will be all right. He needs Jesus' love, and he needs a counselor who can objectively help him to get at the roots of his behavior. You are the least equipped to be objective because you are too emotionally involved with him.

3. *You are not called by anyone, least of all by God, to offer yourself as a punching bag.* Do not listen to the "religious" voices that tell you that you must take whatever comes in order to be a submissive wife. That is a totally warped interpretation of Scripture. (See chapter two, "Women's Liberation in the Bible.")

You are a child of God, His treasure, and you honor Him by esteeming yourself enough in Him to say to an abusive husband, "Your behavior is not acceptable, and I will not allow it because I value my life and because I love you too much to let you continue in this pattern. *I will not enable you* to sow more and more negative seeds that you will eventually reap. Either get the help you need or get out!" Many times, a temporary legal separation has provided the incentive for a reluctant husband to pursue the help he needs, and marriages have been restored to a healthy basis.

4. *Make sure your husband goes to a counselor of* your *choice.* Men left alone often choose counselors they can "con"—and no lasting healing results.

5. *Seek help yourself, preferably from a competent Christian counselor, and become part of a support group.* You have a life to live whether your husband responds or not. You need to deal with whatever may be in your heart that could draw more abuse to you.

6. *Do not confuse tears with repentance.* Watch for "fruit" in his life "in keeping with repentance" (Matt. 3:8; Acts 26:20). Let the counselor tell you when healing has progressed far enough to enable you to be safely together. Otherwise the same pattern will repeat itself again.

### *Learn to navigate through the river of tears.*

I caution you that when you have allowed tears to accomplish their initial tension-releasing, cleansing effect, it is important to turn your attention outward to the concerns of others; otherwise, you build retaining walls of self-pity and drown in the accumulating saltwater.

Even before I specifically invited Jesus to crucify my habits of wallowing in feelings, of private speech-making, and of self-pity, I knew I had to focus my rising energies of hurt and anger as aggressively and positively as I could, or my own fires would consume me. I knew discernment could be warped.

One small incident could be blown up to represent falsely the whole of our marital relationship and trap me in a lie that could become a prison. Or it might express itself like a knife going through me in criticism. An athletic morning of house-cleaning or yard work, or a vigorous bike ride or walk with the children, was often effective for me as a tension releaser. A paintbrush in my hand was an instrument of therapy as well as creativity. The paint stayed where I put it and looked back at me as something beautiful and comforting.

But finding positive outlets for energies was seldom enough. I discovered that if I didn't discipline my thoughts, I could sometimes make up brilliant and increasingly angry speeches to the rhythm of my vacuum cleaner. When I tried to discipline my thoughts in the strength of my own flesh, I wearied myself and lost the battle. So I learned to pray simple, straightforward prayers at the moment I first recognized negative feelings rising in me. An example of such a prayer follows.

> *Lord, I'm angry. I feel like punching him. I feel like I'm right and he's wrong, but I don't know that. Right or wrong, I'm responsible for my feelings and what I do with them. I don't know how to change my feelings. But I choose not to entertain them or feed them, or else they'll grow. I choose not to push them down, because if I do, they'll come back up bigger and stronger. Here they are. Take charge of them and me. Give me Your mind, Your heart, Your feelings, Your response.*
> *P. S. Bless him.*

Then I would go about my business, and God was faithful to do His part. Somewhere in the process, I learned to take personal responsibility for *my* sin and *not* to take personally *every* hurtful word or action that came my way.

## LET NOTHING TERRIFY YOU

There are many passages in the Bible that call you to live in a way that seems extremely difficult and often nearly impossible in the midst of a sinful generation. Not the least of these is 1 Peter 3, which encourages married women to live in a respectful relationship with their husbands:

> ...so that even if any of them are disobedient to the word, they may be won without a word by the behavior of their wives, as they observe your chaste and respectful behavior. And let not your adornment be merely external— braiding the hair, and wearing gold jewelry, or putting on dresses; but let it be the hidden person of the heart, with the imperishable quality of a gentle and quiet spirit, which is precious in the sight of God. For in this way in former times the holy women also, who hoped in God, used to adorn themselves, being submissive to their own husbands. Thus Sarah obeyed Abraham, calling him lord, and you have become her children *if you do what is right without being frightened by any fear.*
> —1 PETER 3:1–6, *emphasis added*

The Amplified Version translates the latter portion of that passage: "...if you do right and let nothing terrify you [not giving way to hysterical fears or letting anxieties unnerve you]." What anxieties are there to unnerve a woman? What is there to terrify her? Paul is not referring to a specific category of battered and abused wives. He is addressing married women in general.

## WHEN YOUR MATE HAS A STONY HEART

Genesis 3:16 tells us that a woman's desire shall be for her husband. This does not refer only to sexual need or desire for security, protection, and prestige. Far more important is her passionate desire to be for him all that she was created to be. She is bone of his bone and flesh of his flesh (Gen. 2:23), a joint-heir with him of the grace of life (God's unmerited favor—1 Pet. 3:7). She is the *one* whom God has provided to nurture and protect his heart (Prov. 31:11). He is the *one* whom God has provided to be the primary human nurture and protection for her.

If your husband has been so wounded in his childhood that he has built reinforced self-protective walls and self-centered coping mechanisms to defend himself—if he has developed a heart of stone (Ezek. 11:19; 36:26) to avoid feeling pain—then he will shut you out. You, in turn, feel rejected and undefended. More importantly, you are not allowed to do what you instinctively know you are designed and called to do, which is to be a comfort to him.

A wall is a wall, and it prevents the good as well as the bad from penetrating. Each time you reach out to your husband and hit the hard walls of his heart, the more rejected and hopeless you feel...the more frustrated, anxious, and perhaps even frantic you become. As you continue to fail in your attempt to break through, you even question your own worth. The loneliness you live with is often felt more keenly in his presence than away from him.

If your stone-hearted husband communicates at all, it is

usually about superficial or peripheral matters. Or, like a turtle, he pops out periodically to test the atmosphere and withdraws quickly into his shell. He diligently avoids vulnerability. Though he may appear on the surface to be kind and giving, he is unable to receive more than carefully controlled tidbits from others.

As his wife, you may live in excruciating loneliness; you may even struggle with jealousy as you see your husband relate easily and considerately with secondary people while you forever wait outside his door. Tragically, he may be totally unaware that he is alienating you and deaf to the true meaning of your pleas as he tells you, "Get off my back," or as he relaxes in the silence of your depression.

I am not talking only about the man who has lost his ability to express his own emotions, nor the one who thinks he is protecting his wife by not sharing his troubles. I am describing a condition of much more serious bondage to fear and compulsion to control.

A person with a hardened heart may rationalize his own behavior and totally reject responsibility for having elicited negative responses from others. The harder his heart becomes, the more he loses an awareness of the effect he has on those closest to him. He perceives their attempts to break through to him as some form of criticism or attack.

Very early in John's life he lived with lacerating criticism. He learned that to find peace he had several alternatives: He could disappear from his home and run off to the barn or into the pasture to enjoy nonthreatening fellowship with his dog, Joy, and his cow, Spring. They never talked back to him, and he could find easy rest and refreshment in their adoring company. He could also hide in the wonderful solitude of the attic and become lost in a book, or he could immerse himself in music.

Often it wasn't possible to disappear, so he developed an efficient skill of tuning out the critical voice of his mother, even while in her presence. This ability, practiced over a long period of time, made it very easy for him to flee quickly into comfortable isolation without even thinking about it.

During the earlier years of our marriage, if challenging strains of "Why...?"— "Where...?"—"Come here..."—"Will you...?"—"Have you...?"—"Are you listening?" (with or without critical overtones) began to fill the air, he was very quickly "gone."

There was rarely anything deliberate about that dynamic. It happened because it had been built in during his formative years and was automatically being projected onto his number-one primary person in the present—me. Of course, the areas of my own sinful nature not yet dealt with often made a significant contribution to the continuation of John's patterns.

Long-practiced habits eventually become automatic and compulsive. What begins as a coping mechanism and a defense for emotional survival can—and usually does—become a prison. Jesus Christ came to set the prisoners free. Learning to receive, to take hold of, and to live in that freedom is a process.

For many years John and I taught what we had learned concerning the heart of stone. John again and again forgave those who needed forgiveness, asked forgiveness for his own heart of stone, and prayed uncounted times that it be melted.

The Lord transformed many areas of my life, also. Yet we became aware that there was a destructive pattern still operating in our lives. Often, when everything had been going unusually well between us, John would manage within a day or two to do something mean and ornery. I would react with hurt and tearful anger. "What did I do? I thought everything was going great!" It didn't make sense to either one of us.

Then the Lord revealed that there were deeper levels of fear to vulnerability in John than we had yet seen. He could handle anything that appeared as an attack. He had built a sturdy defense and a hiding place against perceived attacks. But when goodness, tenderness, and sweetness began to melt the innermost core of his heart, he felt out of control. He had to do *something* to stop the flow of love. Then, if I retaliated with defensiveness, anger, or accusation, he felt justified in withdrawing.

We talked and prayed about the problem together. We prayed that every need to control that existed in either of us be destroyed. I disciplined myself to learn how to better stop my anxious thoughts and take authority over my feelings by telling God about them and by praying instantly for my negative reactions to be crucified. I also learned to resist the tendency to lick my wounds and, instead, to spend that energy praying for John to be blessed with strength of spirit to hold his heart open. John learned how to check his fears and rising impulses to flee and how to take authority over his feelings and pray, "Lord, keep me truly vulnerable."

Healing, transformation, and the melting of a stony heart are all part of a process. John thought this work in him was finally complete when one evening at our kinship group he asked for prayer. He had some needs, and he was also setting an example of vulnerability for the others. Shortly into the prayer time, the group stopped to confront John in love. "John, why is it that when you ask us to pray for you, you very quickly turn the tables on us and start teaching us how, and how much, to minister to you?"

The old issue of fear and the need to control was dealt with again on another level as he forgave his mother—*again*—and received forgiveness for his judgments and resultant coping mechanisms. The group prayed *again* that the old habits would die. John considered them to be dead and, consequently, brought forth a good deal of fruit that would indicate it was so.

But then, years later, the same problem began to appear in different guises. John and I would be on the phone talking with our grown children. The conversations were pleasant, even delightful, but after a short time John would become uneasy and would excuse himself. He had something "important" to do and couldn't talk any longer.

After a few minutes, I would hear a toilet flush and the TV go on. I would try to check my rising irritation and would compensate for his absence by talking all the more enthusiastically with the children. Then I would confront him later about it, asking, "Why?" He would come up with excuses that the Lord let him know were "too noble," and he had to face the truth again. The loving conversations were melting deeper levels of his heart of stone. Once again, he was fleeing from vulnerability.

By this time he had experienced enough healing and received enough strength of spirit that he could take full responsibility for his unconscious choices and reckon the root of the sinful structure dead in himself. Is it finished? It was finished when Christ died on the cross for his sins.

Has John finished taking hold of what Christ accomplished for him? I don't know. But I sincerely and gratefully declare that our relationship is rich, growing, fulfilling, often exciting, and generally peaceful. We are *together* and at rest because we are united in the power of the Lord against a common enemy, our own flesh (and the devil as he tries from time to time to expand whatever areas of sin we may try to hang on to). We no longer fight each other, and the Lord has transformed our struggles of the past to become part of our compassion, wisdom, and gratitude for one another.

## WHEN YOU LOSE TRUST OR RESPECT FOR YOUR MATE

Far more hurtful than trying to share your life with a man who has a heart of stone is being in a marriage with a man who has no moral backbone, no real sense of integrity and truth, no stability, or no faithfulness in which you can rest.

However painfully intense John and I were in our problem solving, we never doubted one another's faithfulness, loyalty, or morality. Nor did we question the *intention* of the other to be honest and considerate. I could still respect my husband as being a man after God's own heart even when he was in his late-bloomer stage, when he was not hearing or heeding me as *I* thought he should, and when he appeared to be controlling and critical. Even during those times when I didn't feel loved and was aggressively angry and defensive, I still respected him. I never really wanted to run him into the ground, and I was relieved when he wouldn't let me do so.

Many women today are married to men who have never grown up emotionally and perhaps never will. These men come from dysfunctional families where basic trust was never established by clean, wholesome, affectionate touch and consistent, loving discipline. They are the shattered products of scattered families, a wounded generation that tends to seek comfort in substance abuse and the accumulation of material wealth.

Many people today struggle with a lost sense of the absoluteness of God's eternal laws. Whatever feels good must be OK, and only the "bigots" talk about what is right or wrong. This present generation has been well indoctrinated with demands for rights rather than being taught about duties and responsibilities. Very few know the meaning of laying down their own lives for the sake of blessing others.

Today's woman is less out of touch with who she is than today's man. Our culture has done more to destroy the role of men than of women, although, clearly, female identity is also being threatened with demolition today. Very few men today have grown up working alongside their fathers, as young men did in previous generations. With today's hectic lifestyle, fathers who devote quality time, affection, and consistent appropriate discipline to their children are extremely rare these days.

Most sons have not had strong, wholesome male role models with whom they can identify. No doubt mothers are important, and a boy's identification with her begins before birth. But if the father is not there for him in a way that communicates security and belonging, he cannot confidently move away from the familiarity of his mother to embrace a world away from her.

A little boy especially needs to develop a secure relationship and identification with his father as he begins to notice the physical difference between his mother and father and begins to separate from her by virtue of his uniqueness. If the father/son relationship is not well established (or if he does not have a relationship with another primary male figure), then male identification is difficult, and his sense of who he is becomes confusing. Women don't have to make that sort of transition. From their conception on, they remain identified with their femininity (unless some trauma disrupts their lives and causes them to reject their identity with their mother).

Though many of today's young men have been denied strong father role models, they have had abundant opportunity to feed on the television "hero" role model who jumps into bed with every female he dates even casually. These young men have grown up with exaltation of the macho figure that never expresses a real emotion about anything.

Most young men have witnessed murder and rape to the point of being desensitized to the horror of it. Pornography is represented as being "adult," condoms as guaranteeing "safe" sex, and reaching the age of twenty-one as being "mature" enough to go out and get drunk. For those who are in a hurry to "grow up," all of these things, plus various drugs, are fairly easily available to schoolchildren.

Who will tell our young men the truth about what it is to be a *real* man? Who will model godly manhood to them so that they can know what it is to be a husband and a father? Who will give them strength of spirit to stand against the destructive forces in our culture? Who will awaken conscience in them? Who will teach them what true love is and how to recognize it? The church is beginning to wake up as the Holy Spirit calls them to the task.

## RISKY BUSINESS

It is scary to think about a woman submitting her life, becoming joined in one flesh, to a man who has been known for womanizing and is still tempted to do so with no remorse or conscience. She lives with the fear that he may show up at some time testing HIV-positive. She feels continually defiled. What is she to do?

Similarly, how can she respect her husband if she knows he is not dealing honestly in business? That he is wasting their resources and not paying bills? How can she truly meet him in their relationship when alcohol or drugs dull his sensitivities? How can she even talk with him about these things when she is afraid of the backlash?

The question, then, is this: What is a woman to do? Let's look at the relationship between Sarah and Abraham and how Sarah interacted with her husband.

Abraham was not always the wise, mature, faith-filled patriarch we are sometimes led to believe. At the beginning of his faith journey, Abraham was immature, foolish, and inconsiderate of his wife, Sarah. He lied not once but twice, declaring Sarah as his sister instead of his wife, jeopardizing not only their relationship but also his wife's very life.

When there was a famine, he and Sarah traveled to Egypt, where he told Sarah to lie about her true identity, declaring her to the Egyptians and Pharaoh as his sister. (See Genesis 12:10–20.) Later on, in Genesis 20, Abraham lied again (for fear that he might be killed), this time to King Abimelech, saying she was his sister, and the king took her into his own house. Abraham's cowardice deliberately put his wife in a compromising position where she could have been forced into adultery.

At that point in his life Abraham was certainly not a husband who would risk himself to protect his wife, and yet Sarah obeyed him. God Himself protected Sarah from the Pharaoh and from Abimelech. Ironically, Abraham's son, Isaac, repeats the same scenario with his wife, Rebekah, and Abimelech in Genesis 26.

What would cause Sarah to submit herself to such a compromising position? It was her trust in God and her relationship with Him that caused her to willingly obey her husband's wishes, even though it might jeopardize her. Look at Peter's words: "And now you are her children if you do right and let nothing terrify you" (1 Pet. 3:6, RSV). In other words, women, like Sarah, can dare to give themselves into the care of an immature, self-centered, untrustworthy husband only if they have developed a strong enough relationship with God.

Too many women expect too much from their husbands and lean too heavily on them, asking them to do what only *God* can do. "It is better to take refuge in the LORD than to trust in man. It is better to take refuge in the LORD than to trust in princes" (Ps. 118:8–9). "Do not trust in princes, in mortal man, in whom there is no salvation" (Ps. 146:3).

Every man (and woman) is an arm of flesh, and an arm of flesh will fail you at some time or another. Only God Himself can be trusted to relate to you perfectly. God alone is able to sort out a husband's errors, rebuke him appropriately, and redeem the effects of sin.

There is no guarantee that your husband will ever change, even if your behavior reflects the righteousness of God and you have all the faith in the world. God never forces anyone to receive anything, but He will move powerfully upon the hearts of His children if we allow Him. Therefore, you need to first develop a growing relationship with the Lord so that you will gain in strength and power and know how to stand when the time comes.

If your strength is first of all in God, you can then be appropriately dependent on your husband and at the same time properly independent. Jesus says, "If anyone comes to Me, and does not hate his own father and mother and wife [or husband] and children and brothers and sisters, yes, and even his own life, he cannot be My disciple" (Luke 14:26). Of course, Jesus does not call us to *hate* in the sense of strong destructive emotions directed toward people. He has called us to *love* even our enemies.

What He calls us to hate is the continuing carnal influence and fleshly ties and loyalties that keep us from giving Him first place in our lives. As we cut free from emotional bondages and learn to follow Jesus, we are enabled to love as He loves and see ourselves—and others—as He sees.

## WHAT DO WE DO WITH FEARS AND FEELINGS?

Part of learning to love your husband is learning to give each other space from time to time. It's healthy for you and your marital relationship. As a woman, learn to develop outside interests not dependent on your husband so that your strength is renewed when it's time to come together. If you're not married, you still need friends. As women, our friendships with other women are vitally important. We need the fellowship of a few close friends with whom we can talk, laugh, and cry—people with whom we share common interests and who know how to enjoy life.

You will also benefit greatly from regular exercise, music, and good books. Take some time to hone a skill, whatever it may be—sewing, painting, crafts, writing. The ideal situation is for you to become grounded in the nurturing and supportive fellowship of a good, Bible-believing church. Use wisdom when scheduling your "time out" to avoid a conflict with your husband's need to be with you. Otherwise he will feel like he's competing for your attention and, as a result, become jealous.

So how do we avoid giving way to hysterical fears, not letting anxieties unnerve us? God's Word is clear:

> Cast your burden upon the LORD, and He will sustain you;
> He will never allow the righteous to be shaken.
> —PSALM 55:22

Your necessary righteous discipline is to cast your burden on the Lord when you first become aware of it, before it has the opportunity to take firm hold of you. Don't entertain it. Don't wallow in it. Don't feed it with resentment and bitterness. Acknowledge it, offer it to the Lord, release it, affirm your identity in Him, and go about your business.

*Chapter 4*

# A TIME *for* GRIEF *and* SORROW

E VERYONE, REGARDLESS OF THEIR status, experiences sorrow and grief at some point in their life.
These two emotions are an inescapable part of living.
According to Webster's dictionary, *sorrow* implies a sense of
loss, guilt, or remorse, while *grief* implies poignant sadness for
an immediate cause.

Grief may last a long time when we lose someone we care
about—especially one who never knew the Lord. To receive
comfort from Jesus in such a case involves repeated choices
to lay down our fears, judgments, and unanswered questions.
It means trusting in God's ability to run His universe in love,
justice, and mercy.

Grief may be quickly healed following the loss of loved ones
who you know have gone to be with the Lord. You have wept for
them, but now you rejoice for them. You have faith to believe
that someday you will be reunited with them. Yet sorrow may
surge up into tears at unexpected times when memories are

triggered or when treasured new events happen in your life that you can no longer share with your loved one. There's a sense of loss or remorse. Your tears of sorrow are a natural, healthy reaction and are nothing to be ashamed of. Let them flow. Tell the Lord about your feelings, and go on about your business. Don't try to suppress your feelings; emotional volcanoes are built that way.

## WHEN A PARENT DIES

When we grieve the death of a parent, it is particularly painful because, deep down, we know that no one can ever take the place of a parent. The pain of that loss is unique to your situation, and God is the only one who can give you genuine comfort. Let me share with you my personal experience with grief and sorrow.

### *Losing a father*

My father was a hero figure in my life. When we lost my father to Alzheimer's disease, it devastated our family; however, it was particularly difficult for me.

As a traveling salesman, his job required him to be gone from home a great deal, but when he came home to his family, he was 100 percent with us. I was the oldest of five children, and we always anticipated his Friday homecomings and spending the weekend with him before he had to leave again early Monday morning. We would wait excitedly for him to walk through the door with that familiar grin on his face, his arms outstretched to share hugs. Mother would come out of the kitchen to greet him warmly, then scurry back to finish preparing dinner.

The most memorable part of our weekend with Dad was our Sunday afternoon trips around St. Louis and the surrounding countryside after attending church. Driving the car again was the last thing a traveling salesman wanted to do, but he knew that we loved it. The crowning point of each adventure was that we were given the privilege of choosing what delicious thing we each wanted to buy with our five cents. (For the younger generation, during the Depression and even post-Depression days, this was a luxury!)

On Sunday evenings Dad always had to spend time typing his job reports before leaving the next morning. Whenever we asked him a question, he never seemed to be upset that we interrupted his typing. He would slowly look up from his work, his dentures hanging out the corner of his mouth for our amusement, and, with a twinkle in his quizzical eyes, ask, "What now?" If we came crashing by in an argumentative or rambunctious hassle, he would settle the disturbance with the justly stern but quiet reprimand we knew we deserved.

With Dad on the road most of the time, Mother had to be the principal disciplinarian because she was home with us full-time. Sometimes it got to be a bit too much for her emotions to handle. But Dad was a calm, consistent, solid support beneath her, and we knew it.

My parents retired at the same time, he from sales and she from teaching, and spent a number of years doing many things they hadn't been able to do together when Dad was traveling and Mom was too busy running the household.

It was painful for all of us when Dad developed Alzheimer's disease. We watched helplessly as the lovable and dependable rock we had known slowly cracked and crumbled. The man who had always had a sense of direction would suddenly find himself lost in familiar places and would have to ask for help in order to get home. That was bewildering and humiliating for him.

He had always been top salesman for his company, largely because of his ability to communicate ideas as well as his charming integrity. Now, simple words would suddenly be lost from his vocabulary, and he would stop in the middle of a sentence, not knowing what to say, a furtive look rising in his eyes as he struggled to get hold of the right word for articles as common as "table" and "bread."

When it first began to happen, if we could supply the missing word, his eyes would brighten, and he would laugh as he continued. But he grew more and more frustrated in trying to express himself and would sometimes quietly throw up his hands, tears welling up in his eyes.

He gradually lost track of time and would get out of bed at all hours of the night. Mom became afraid to go to sleep for fear that he might wander outside. The simple functions of table utensils became a mystery to him, and he lost the ability to dress himself properly. But he never lost the desire to be helpful around the house and persisted in continually reorganizing things in strange ways and places.

Mom was exhausting herself, but she was determined that as long as her beloved husband was able to recognize people, she would take care of him at home. When she slipped on the ice and fell on the way to the mailbox and had to have surgery for a complete hip replacement, it seemed to us that God had intervened and taken the decision out of her hands.

My brother Jerry and sister Sue decided to place Dad in a Christian nursing home, explaining carefully to him that Mother was in the hospital and would be all right, but she would not be able to care for him at home anymore. He couldn't put it all together, but he did grasp with great anxiety that she had been injured. After she recovered and came to see him nearly every afternoon, he would embrace her, pat her gently, touch the walker that she used for a while, and strain with questions and concern for her that he couldn't put into words.

We brought him a little book with all the pictures of his family in it, and he carried it with him wherever he went. From the evidence of tears on some of the pages, I believe he wept over the photos at times. The staff asked my mother again and again, "Has he always been such a kind man? Usually these patients become belligerent! But Paul is always so kind!"

It is difficult to describe the feelings that beset me as I watched my father become increasingly lost from himself and us. One day when I came to St. Louis to visit, we walked together up and down the corridor, arm in arm, numerous times. His walk was a halting shuffle. But when he saw a patient heading directly toward us in a wheelchair, from somewhere inside this man who had been leaning heavily on me to keep his balance came a momentary surge of strength—he pulled me out of the path of the wheelchair.

I was nearly overwhelmed: first, by the undying protective love in my dad and, second, with the realization of how the power of love enables the mind and body to rise above their physical limitations to accomplish impossible tasks.

When I left my father that day, we hugged each other for a long time and cried together; I told him how precious he was, how much we all loved him, and how proud I was of him. He walked with me as far as the fence, which separated the patients from the elevator door, quietly smiled through his tears, and watched with deep sadness in his eyes as I walked into the elevator. When the door shut and no one was there, I collapsed into sobs.

It is a wonder that I made it to my parents' home safely through city traffic amid the torrent of tears flooding my eyeballs. I was up front with God about my feelings—"I am so hurt for him—and so angry! He was so good—and he gave so much—and he finally had time to rest and enjoy life! He and Mom had to be satisfied with weekend fellowship in their marriage for so many years! Why this? Why couldn't they live out the rest of their lives together? They don't deserve this! It doesn't seem fair!" I went on and on.

And God just listened. I knew He was hearing with compassion. When I had poured out enough of the pain, I continued to pray, "Lord, have mercy on him. Please, will You either heal him completely or take him home to be with You? But I earnestly pray You release his beautiful spirit from the prison of his deteriorating mind and body. Let him know he hasn't been abandoned here in this place. Take him into Your house, Lord, and into Your arms, and wipe away all his tears. Fill him with Your healing love. Lord, he never really knew what it was to have a father, and yet he did a good job of fathering anyhow. Let him come into his inheritance with You. Let him *know You*, Father, and give him comfort and joy. Let him know how much we all love him and how much we appreciate the many ways he laid down his life for us."

The more I cried and prayed, the better I felt. A peace settled into my innermost being. Something inside of me let go. I didn't strive emotionally anymore to make something happen that was beyond my control. I didn't have to wrestle with my feelings any longer, or with guilt for things I had done or left undone in relation to him as I was growing up. I wasn't plagued any longer with unanswered questions.

I returned home to Idaho into a busy ministry schedule and continued to send frequent picture-postcards with simple bits of news and "I love you" messages. I knew Dad's spirit could still understand and needed the touch of my love again and again. I prayed that God would comfort and nurture him in the depths of his spirit.

God answered my prayer. Later I learned that others in the family had been praying similarly. In a short time Dad had a series of small strokes and went home to be with the Father. He didn't have to go through all the debilitating stages of Alzheimer's disease. He never lost his ability to recognize relatives and close friends who came to visit. He never completely lost his sense of humor. He never ceased to be kind.

We all wept at his passing, though not for long. It was sweet sorrow, and the weeping was largely for us. Our dad was gone. We would miss him. Mostly we rejoiced for him; he had been let out of prison, set free to be and express those qualities with which he had blessed us for so many years—more uninhibitedly and purposefully than ever before.

The grief we experienced was overcome by the celebration of joy and gratitude for his being released to go to the Father.

### Losing a mother

Very soon after my father died, Mother accompanied John, our daughter Andrea, and me on a trip to Israel and five countries in Europe. She was wise enough to know she needed to fill her days with forward-looking, life-giving activities. In Israel our group did an unusual amount of walking, and the hip replacement she had received gave her some discomfort, but she didn't want to miss anything. She wanted everything God wanted for her.

The only hill she couldn't climb was the heights of Masada when the gondola was broken, and she declined that challenge primarily because she didn't want to slow us down. She had grown accustomed to costing herself whatever pain was necessary in order to do what she counted joyous and important.

At the time of our daughter Ami's wedding, Mom was excited and enthusiastic as she visited in the homes of all her grandchildren and great-grandchildren. She helped with the wedding preparations, decorating and making salad and sandwiches. She worked alongside the rest of us as we set up chairs for the reception, and she delighted in visiting with all the guests. When she mentioned later that she was feeling a little tired, we suggested that she rest, but no one had cause for concern or alarm.

A week and a half after she returned home from her visit, she died of acute leukemia. Even the doctor did not suspect anything serious and at first had only treated her at home for what he thought were merely flu symptoms. When she became too exhausted to talk on the telephone, my sister took her to the hospital.

John and I were taping a series of videos at a TV station in Winnipeg, Canada, when we received a call that Mom's condition was improving. We finished the videos in an afternoon marathon, and then John flew to a conference in Dallas where we were scheduled to speak. I flew to St. Louis to be with my mother and with the rest of my family who had come from various parts of the United States.

Expecting to find her improved, I was shocked to find her in a comatose state. Two of my brothers shared that they believed she could hear us, that a little earlier in the day they had said to her that they were going to get some lunch. She had roused a moment, pointed to her purse, and said, "There's some money in there." That gesture had almost wiped them out—nearly comatose on her deathbed, she was still thinking of their welfare!

My brother Stan was the last to arrive at the hospital, and I said to our mother, "Every one of your children are here now, Mom." She wasn't able to answer, but we all visited quietly, and in a very short while she let go and was gone.

The nurse said, "Her vital signs were so weak I couldn't understand what was keeping her alive. She must have been waiting for you." We all sat in stunned silence. My brother Norman was kneeling at her bedside, and I believe we were all praying silently. But not one of us was praying with any of the ease with which we usually had been able to pray for others.

I couldn't take hold of my thoughts. *O God, bless her,* was all I could put together; I felt as if I could explode with emotion but had no way to let it out. It was as if I were suspended helplessly. I desperately wanted to do something, but I didn't know what it was or how to get hold of it.

We were, for a time, a unit of intense loneliness. Then we got up, hugged one another, and walked out silently, pausing for a moment to thank the nurse for her kindness to our mother. She replied, her eyes swimming with tears, "She ministered to me."

It was a quiet evening, and the Lord unplugged gushers of pent-up emotion in the privacy of our bedrooms. I was then easily able to pray blessing and release, and I fell asleep with an awareness of the comforting presence of God.

The pastor came to visit and asked simply that we tell him about our mother. We had a good time sharing the precious memories we had. Then the pastor shared with us some things that we hadn't known. At eighty-three years of age, Mother was still active in ministry. Her passing meant he would have to find a number of people to replace her in the life of the church.

We all agreed that we had expected her to live forever, and we saw that she had been the glue that held our far-flung family together.

When my husband, John, first arrived for the funeral and saw Mom in the casket, he was puzzled. Then he realized why. In all the thirty-seven years we had been married, he had never seen her lying down. She was always busy serving others!

At her funeral, the pastor shared with everyone what we had told him and summed it all up by reading the closing refrain of a poem I had written years before for my parent's fiftieth wedding anniversary celebration:

> Some plan and scheme and push as children grow—
> And bind their offspring to them as they go
> In selfish striving.
> But Mother launched her dreams from ironing boards,
> And blessed their rising.

We all stayed for a few days, visiting together and dispensing household belongings so my sister would not have the whole burden of settling the estate. We comforted one another with positive remarks about how glad we were that both parents had lived long, full lives, how wonderful it was that our mother's prayer never to be a burden to anyone was fulfilled, what a rich legacy we had been left, and the like. Our conversation was a healing balm at the time, and we meant what we were saying— but it did not do away with what we would all find ourselves experiencing in the months to come.

John and I left within a week for a monthlong trip to many churches in Scotland, Wales, and England. I felt reasonably settled and comforted inside. My full attention was focused on the work at hand. Then our youngest daughter, Andrea, telephoned us in Paisley, Scotland, to tell us that she and Randy were planning to be married during Christmas. I put the phone down and began to share the news excitedly with John.

But a sudden rush of deep sorrow overwhelmed me, and

I delivered the joyful news through a stream of tears. It had dawned on me that I couldn't call my parents to share the good news about their granddaughter! I hadn't been aware of the emotion still needing release from deep inside of me. Later, near Lancaster, England, as John and I were walking alone beside a beautiful river, I experienced the same overwhelming flood of sorrow. John comforted me and helped me realize that I had been so completely occupied with others' needs that I had neglected my own need to work through the grieving process completely. We shared our mutual feelings of sorrow, and it felt good.

I had buried my feelings of guilt for having been so emotionally paralyzed and prevented from audible prayer at my mother's death. At the rational level, I knew there was nothing any of us *could* have done. But at the emotional level, I needed the assurance of forgiveness. Later, the sorrow arose again with the joyful birth of three new grandbabies. By this time, however, I had learned what is comforting to me to do instantly with such feelings. It is so simple: "Jesus, I can't share the good news with them, but You can. Will You please deliver a message?"

## WHEN A HUSBAND DIES

It is natural to grieve and experience sorrow for a time after the death of an aging parent. But it is far more intense when a husband dies.

Hopefully, by the time a woman marries, she has become her own person and has cut free from the emotional attachment to her parents in order to truly become one flesh with her husband (Gen. 2:24; Eph. 5:31; Ps. 45:10). The dynamics of the parent/child relationship change and involve loving and caring for parents, free of childhood loyalties and dependencies.

As a married woman, of course, you will feel a great sense of loss when your parents die. But you should have already experienced as an adult, and further as a married woman, letting go of them as primary supporters, affirmers, protectors, providers, confidants, and advisors. Your husband is more than primary *to* you; he is one flesh *with* you. Therefore, your parents' passing contains far less trauma than the loss of your husband.

When your husband dies, you feel torn apart inside, as if a part of you has died with him. The reason is because you were bone of his bone and flesh of his flesh (Gen. 2:23). You shared a degree of intimacy within your marriage that was blessed—body, mind, heart, and spirit. All the spiritual faith and emotional strength in the world will not deter the pain you will experience.

On the other hand, God's Word comforts you: "Blessed are those who mourn, for they *shall* be comforted" (Matt. 5:4, emphasis added). God also "*heals* the brokenhearted, and binds up their wounds" (Ps. 147:3, emphasis added). Emotional healing does not usually transpire instantly. God respects your feelings and your need to grieve for a while. He knows when you are willing to receive from Him and when you are ready to emotionally let go of a loved one and get on with your life. He longs to pour the balm of His Spirit into your wounds like a medicine, but He waits for your invitation.

> The LORD *longs to be gracious to you*, and therefore He waits on high to have compassion on you. For the LORD is a God of justice; how *blessed are all those who long for Him.*
>
> —ISAIAH 30:18, *emphasis added*

When you invite Him to heal your emotions, think of your prayer like turning on a faucet. The water pressure is already there; the water flows out to fill your cup when you turn on the tap. If you hold a full cup under the faucet and turn the faucet on, at first the cup will not hold the water. If you persist in holding the cup there, soon the steady pressure of the water will displace what was in your cup. It is the same with your grief.

If your innermost being is filled to the brim with grief, do not wait until the grief is gone to offer yourself to the Lord in prayer. You may sit for a very long time with a cup you are unwilling or afraid to share with Him, and its contents will become bitter. Offer your cup as it is, now, and choose to trust God to pour His water with the measure of power He knows is best for you.

No doubt, it is very difficult to pray while experiencing intense emotion. But even during such times of intense emotional pain, it has been comforting for me to read:

> The Spirit also helps our weakness; for we do not know how to pray as we should, but *the Spirit Himself intercedes for us with groanings too deep for words*; and He who searches the hearts knows what the mind of the Spirit is, because He intercedes for the saints according to the will of God.
> —ROMANS 8:26–27, *emphasis added*

So I encourage you to relax and open your heart to Jesus as best you can. Choose to trust that God is ultimately in charge and will cause all things to work together for good (Rom. 8:28).

Some within the body of Christ have said that Christians should not grieve at all and have quoted the following scripture as their "proof" text:

> But we do not want you to be uninformed, brethren, about those who are asleep, that you may not grieve, as do the rest who have no hope. For if we believe that Jesus died and rose again, even so God will bring with Him those who have fallen asleep in Jesus.
>
> —1 THESSALONIANS 4:13–14

This passage is not saying that we will not or should not grieve *at all.* Rather, it says that if we understand what the death and resurrection of Jesus mean, we will not grieve in the same way as people who have no hope in Jesus. We will experience pain as we are separated from those we love. But the substance of our hope is that we know we will someday be reunited with them in Him. Separation is temporary. Comfort is continually available.

Grief is soon healed by prayer. Sorrow will linger awhile. You may be cleaning out a closet and find an old sweater of his—sudden tears surprise you. You put it on and wear it around the house awhile because it feels good. An advertisement comes in the mail addressed to him. A wave of sadness hits you and perhaps even a tiny flicker of anger. "Don't they know he's not here anymore?"

Then come the holidays. Thanksgiving and then Christmas arrive, and you sit down to enjoy a sumptuous meal with your family. You find yourself remembering past holidays when he was there at the head of the table, and for a moment you feel very lonely—even in the midst of loved ones. Such waves of sorrow are to be expected for a time. Don't be embarrassed or impatient with yourself when you experience them. Don't apologize for tears.

But neither should you allow your feelings to rule the day. Let your feelings live, acknowledging them silently to the Lord, giving Him charge over you. Then turn to focus on the joyful reason for the holiday, and pour yourself as best you can into fellowship with family and friends. Life continues on this planet, and God calls you to invest your life here as fully as possible until He calls you to leave.

Some people make the mistake of trying to develop another primary relationship too soon after the death of a spouse. A hole inside begs to be filled. Nothing seems to fully comfort that aching loneliness. Maybe you took for granted your husband's care of household details such as insurance, bills, car maintenance, and investments. Even though you may be intimidated at first by the challenges, with good counsel you can equip yourself with sufficient knowledge to cope. But you find it tremendously difficult and exhausting to live with the emptiness you feel. You can fill your days with busyness, but the nights are long, and television can be depressing company.

Even if your relationship with God is good and vital, you still desire close companionship: love with skin on it—touches and hugs.

Friends with the best of intentions try to be there for you. They still invite you to group gatherings that used to mean so much to you and your husband. But he isn't there anymore, and the fellowship isn't the same. You appreciate the love of your friends and their desire to include you, but you feel somehow awkward without him.

If you rush out to try to fill the void with anything (or anybody) but God's presence and the support of friends for a period of at least two years until you are healed, you are likely to reap heartache. It will be extremely difficult to relate to a new mate with your *whole* being. You need time to cut free emotionally from whatever quality of oneness you experienced with your late husband.

Expect memories to surface frequently, especially if your

marriage was a blessed and fulfilling one. It will be difficult to shed expectations formed by the familiar, satisfying, and comfortable ways blessings have come to you in the past. You could easily, without intending to do so, make comparisons that could fall as judgment and burden on a new spouse. Worse, such comparisons could be expressed unconsciously from hidden places in your heart.

Your familiar and practiced identifications of love need time to die. And a new relationship, if it is to have a healthy future, must develop from a base of mutual friendship and sharing rather than the pressures of need.

When you are overcome with waves of sadness and memories of the loved one you recently lost, allow yourself to do the following:

- Cry your tears.

- Take your quiet times to sort out memories; express your gratitude, regrets, hurts, angers, fears, and needs to the Lord—unpolished.

- Invite Jesus' comfort and healing. Let Him love you.

- Let others pray for you and with you.

- Release your loved one to God the Father, in prayer.

- Choose life.

- Spend time doing things you have always enjoyed.

    ✑    Seek the company of those with whom you
           feel comfortable.

    ✑    Listen to music, whatever sort lifts your spirit.

    ✑    Turn outward to help others.

Don't be dismayed when emotions rise from time to time. And don't be disturbed when people fail to understand. God knows your heart and will persist to draw your residue of sorrow to Himself.

*Chapter 5*

# DEALING WITH *the*
# LOSS *of a* CHILD

H ONEY, SOMETHING IS NOT right with this pregnancy," Mary says.

"What do you mean?" her husband replies.

"I mean, I feel like I'm losing the baby. The obstetrician said that spot bleeding in the first trimester is normal, but something doesn't *feel* right."

A couple of days later, she visits her doctor, and her worst fears are confirmed. "Mrs. Smith, I am so sorry, but you are miscarrying. This is common considering you're over thirty-five, you're approximately eight weeks pregnant, and you've had one previous miscarriage. Please take this material home with you and read it carefully; it should answer most of your questions. Of course, you can call me if you still have questions. If you experience any severe pain, high-grade fever, and the like, please call us immediately and then go to the nearest emergency room. Once your body miscarries the baby, please save the tissue in a container and bring it in so we can send it to a laboratory for testing."

She immediately calls her husband and breaks the news. "We lost the baby!"

"What?" he asks in disbelief.

"I miscarried again!" Then the silence. "Well, aren't you going to say anything?"

Angry, she hangs up the phone. Feeling alone and emotionally numb from the news she just received, she drives home. Amid the flood of tears, thoughts race through her mind: *Tissue? Labs? Did he just say I'm miscarrying? How could he sit there and tell me that so matter-of-factly? Why is he referring to my baby as "tissue"? What did I do wrong this time?*

Meanwhile, on the other side of town, a father is burying his ten-year-old son today.

"God, why couldn't You give *me* the cancer? Why did Jake have to die? He was only ten! He had his whole life ahead of him! I'm angry with You, God. I shouldn't be burying my child today. My son should have buried me!"

Perhaps you can identify with one of these scenarios. Or maybe at one time you were pregnant, but it was an inconvenient time for you to become pregnant for whatever reason. You decided to abort the baby, and now the guilt haunts you.

Whatever your particular situation, there is probably no greater emotional pain than grieving the loss of a child. Some have described it as losing a part of their identity, because each child carries traits of each parent.

Regardless of the length of time a child exists, God has a plan—a *perfect* plan—for each child. God's *perfect* plan is clearly expressed in His Word:

Behold, children are a gift of the LORD; the fruit of the womb is a reward. Like arrows in the hand of a warrior, so are the children of one's youth. How blessed is the *man* whose quiver is full of them.

—PSALM 127:3–5, *emphasis added*

After the birth of our sixth child, I can remember reading those words and thinking, *Whose quiver is full? Who is carrying all these babies anyhow?* Our older children, delighted with the tiny golden redhead who had just joined our family, were already including as their contribution to our table grace, "...and please, God, let Mom have another baby."

I told John I'd be happy to let *him* be pregnant with number seven if God should decide to bless his quiver again. Now I know and understand this verse means that *we* receive blessing. And we *have*, in unbelievable measure, as our children have followed in our spiritual footsteps, taking ever larger, faster, and more gracefully productive steps than we ever did.

Thankfully, I have never lost a child, though I have experienced the anxiety of repeated threats of losing one. Loren entered this world in a drugged state because of ether the doctor gave me (without anyone's permission). Ami was conceived as a tubal pregnancy. Mark threatened for several weeks to miscarry. Johnny was born with an unusually long umbilical cord partially wrapped around his neck. And I had to stay in bed for six weeks to avoid miscarrying Tim.

When I was in labor with Andrea, the doctor tried to break the water, only to find out there was none. Andrea slipped sideways and the umbilical cord wrapped around her, causing her heart rate to drop. The doctor managed to turn her into proper position and literally *pull* her into the world safely.

I am well acquainted with anxiety and fervent prayer, as well as relief and gratitude. I can identify with mothers who have lost their babies, because I know I would have been crushed if I had lost any one of ours, early or late. I know I would have wrestled intently with the questions, "What did I do wrong? What could I have done differently?"

## THE GUILT AND BLAME FOR MISCARRIAGES

It is natural for you to wonder if you are in some way responsible for a miscarriage. But guilt feelings are usually inappropriate. There are reasons why a miscarriage occurred. There are natural, physical causes why you involuntarily aborted the baby.

Miscarriages do not happen because you have a fight with your husband, because you are overtired, because you are upset about finances, or because you are tense after a prolonged and difficult visit from your mother-in-law.

Your doctor is not just trying to make you feel better when he tells you that miscarriage is nature's way of sloughing a defective embryo. He is telling you the truth. Some of the causes for early miscarriage are: fetal abnormalities that would not allow survival, undeveloped fertilized eggs, high fever, or fibroid tumors in the uterus or an oddly formed uterus, both of which would mean too little space for the baby to develop. Later miscarriages can happen because of placental insufficiency that failed to function adequately in servicing the baby, or because of a weak cervix that begins to dilate long before it should.

Sometimes there are underlying spiritual reasons for a miscarriage, although rare. It sometimes happens that women who have had several abortions earlier in life have trouble carrying a child later; the body has received a repeated message—"abort"—and now it obeys spontaneously. In such a case, forgiveness and healing are needed.

We have ministered to a number of women who were so wounded as children that they hated being children. Consciously or unconsciously, from a base of fear and anger, they vowed never to bring a child into such a troubled and hateful world. Now, as adults, they may consciously want to have children, but their inner computer is programmed not to produce or sustain life. Either they have difficulty conceiving, or they miscarry repeatedly for no identifiable physical reasons.

If you are such a person, you need to *do* some forgiving of those who abused you. Fear, still alive in you at deep levels, needs to be ministered to by repeated prayers (preferably by someone else) for comfort, love, inner strength, and protection. God hears us the first time we pray. But our own inner being, like a little child, needs to hear messages of affirmation again and again before we can come to rest and trust. Following that, any possible inner vows not to produce life should be broken in prayer by someone who understands authority in the name of Jesus. By the same authority, the body should be directed to produce life and sustain it, according to God's original plan.

If you have experienced the disappointment of many miscarriages, you may have learned to perceive each regular menstrual period as the loss of a baby and an occasion to grieve. If that is the case, you then need to discipline yourself to choose life and face forward, regardless of your emotions, and to take hold of the healing ministered to you by others.

The prevailing sinful conditions of our culture also contribute to an increasing incidence of miscarriage. Chapter 9 of Hosea speaks of the grossness of the nation's iniquity, their deep depravity, their coming to Baal-peor, and their devoting themselves to shame. Verse 11 says, "...their glory will fly away like a bird—no birth, no pregnancy, and no conception!" Verse 14 says, "Give them a miscarrying womb and dry breasts."

This is a time in history when belief in the absoluteness of the laws of God has been eroded even from the hearts of many Christians. Sin is taken far too lightly. A man who knows "how to possess his own vessel in sanctification and honor, not in lustful passion" (1 Thess. 4:4–5) is rare. Hosea's words apply to us today as well as to the nation of Israel more than 2,700 years ago.

This does not necessarily mean that those who are experiencing miscarriages today are reaping for their own sin. We are a corporate body. We all reap blessings from the labors of people all over the world. We also reap for the sins of mankind.

> He causes His sun to rise on the evil and the good, and sends rain on the righteous and the unrighteous.
> —MATTHEW 5:45

We all need to repent for the sexual sins of our culture, as well as for our own individual transgressions, and pray earnestly for the protection and blessing of our children.

### *Go ahead and grieve*

If you have experienced a miscarriage, allow yourself to grieve for your lost baby. Don't try to comfort yourself by rationalizing, "Well, it doesn't matter; it didn't really have a chance to become a person. It's not really the same as losing a baby." Your baby was a person from the moment of conception. Even if you never felt your child move in your womb, the loss can be emotionally shattering.

Allow your feelings to live. Share them with your husband.

If he hasn't yet really experienced the reality of the pregnancy, he may not have the same feelings of loss you do. If he seems detached, it doesn't mean he doesn't care. It doesn't necessarily mean he never really wanted a baby. Ask him to listen and comfort you anyway. If he can't do that, talk with a woman friend who has gone through the same experience.

Cry your tears. Release to the Lord the little person you have lost, with your blessing, and look forward to a happier day when a healthy conception will be brought to full term. Relax. If you work too hard at trying to make that day happen, you will ruin the spontaneity and blessedness of sexual union with your husband, and your increasing tension will decrease your chances of becoming pregnant again.

### Beauty for ashes

God sometimes graces the sorrowful with comforting assurances beyond their faith.

I'm reminded of a friend of mine who shared a beautiful testimony with me. She had gone through a series of deeply emotional, disturbing experiences that included many personal struggles with persecution and rejection, the death of a family member, and then, finally, a miscarriage, which was devastating to her hopes and dreams. All of these events hit her within the same period of time.

Though she was a new Christian, her relationship with the Lord was healthy. She worked through forgiveness and the pain of grief and loss as well as she was able to do. But guilt feelings that she had never been able to give her lost baby anything but sorrow and death continued to trouble and oppress her. She struggled with her feelings for nearly four years, impatient with her inability to let go and come to rest.

Then, one day, as she and her pastor were praying about the matter, he asked her what she would say to her baby if she could.

"Go on; put your feelings into words, as if your baby were right here. Tell her how you feel about her, what you wish you could have done together," the pastor said.

She did just that, and as they resumed their prayers, God gave her a clear vision of her little girl's face in heaven and opened her ears to hear her child's laughter. Not only that, but she heard peals of laughter from many children. At that moment she was able to let go of the grief she had carried for so long, knowing now, by the Lord's confirming gift, that her child had received life and happiness, not death.

God does not call us to build theologies on such testimonies. Neither does He call us to try to reproduce the same scenario as a comforting technique. God will bring His gifts of comfort and healing to each one in the particular ways and times He chooses.

## WORKING THROUGH THE HEARTACHE OF STILLBIRTH

No amount of loving and sympathetic care and comfort can completely take away the suffering you experience when your child is stillborn, even though Jesus surely bears your grief and carries your sorrows (Isa. 53:4), and friends and family want to give you support and comfort. You are not alone in your pain, grief, nagging guilt, and fear, though you may experience excruciating loneliness.

People who are close to you reach out to help, not knowing what you are ready to hear or receive. Some have the wisdom to wait silently, loving you, empathetically burden-bearing with you, listening when you want to talk. Others, like Job's comforters, may offer absurdly inappropriate advice such as: "Put it behind you." "Cheer up; you can have another baby later." "Don't cry; your baby is better off in heaven." Or they may insensitively pile emotional burdens on you, which are impossible to handle at this time, with admonitions to take thought of your husband or concentrate on the needs of your other children. Sometimes those on the hospital staff are gifted with godly wisdom, love, and sensitivity. Sometimes they are not. Many will avoid mentioning the subject because they are having trouble handling their own feelings of helplessness to save your baby.

Whatever the reactions and capabilities of people around you, your own grieving is a very personal and intimate matter that only the Lord can understand—and at first you may not be able to receive what even *He* has to give. You may be too emotionally numb with shock to feel God's presence or to be open to receive any kind of comfort from people who are attending to you. You may be struggling with anger—most often projected upon the medical staff who failed to warn or prepare you. Perhaps you can't shake the feeling that some tremendous error may have been committed.

You keep thinking, *Why me? Why, God, did You let this happen to* me? *It's not fair! People who don't even want babies have them. Lots of people abuse them, and some even abandon or kill them! I just want a baby to love!*

Sometimes when people come near to help, everything in you screams to be left alone. And sometimes when you *are* left alone, you feel abandoned.

There are no easy solutions. The grieving process can't be hurried or avoided. If you delay the process by denial, suppression, or overcompensation (by hyper-faith or strength of will), then grief, or the stressful effects of *not* grieving, may overwhelm you later.

*Give yourself permission to grieve.* If you are an emotional mess for a time, it does not mean that you are weak. If you allow yourself to grieve, you will come out of the mess much faster.

If your husband is able to weep with you, hold you, and communicate that the two of you can and will work it out together, that is wonderful! I remember how my brother Jerry grieved when he and his wife lost their first baby.

But many men have been falsely taught by our culture that strong men don't cry. So their practiced response to emotional pain may be to exercise self-control and appear to be matter-of-fact, or to suppress and withdraw, or to get very busy with things they can manage in order to feel competent.

They may even believe what they are doing is necessary to support you or to be strong for the sake of the rest of the family. Some may find some inanimate thing to punch in order to relieve stress, or may explode spontaneously on any person who happens to be in the vicinity. If your husband's reaction is in any way inappropriate to your feelings or your need, do not assume that he is not as pained as you. As isolated and rejected as you may feel, refuse to accept and feed your nagging thoughts that perhaps he does not love you, or that he *means* to abandon you when you need him the most.

Depression following the loss of your baby is very likely. Try to understand that your body has poured tremendous energy into the nurturing of that little one for the full term of your pregnancy. Your excitement has mounted with anticipation of fulfillment of beautiful hopes and dreams. Now that there is no baby to nurture, your system snaps like an overstretched rubber band. But unlike the rubber band, when you have rested and grieved your grief, you *will* rise again and regain resilience.

You may experience sexual problems for a while, but don't worry about yourself or doubt your love for your husband. It is very difficult to experience sexual stimulation or pleasure when you are feeling depressed. Don't worry about yourself if you do begin to experience some pleasure and then feel a rush of tears. Know that this is a normal part of the process of coming back up again.

If you find yourself struggling with dreams about giving birth to a stillborn or damaged child, don't jump to interpret such a dream as a prophetic warning. It is probably no more than open emotional wounds, fears, or guilt arising from your subconscious. Never suppress fears. Let them surface where they can be faced and overcome. Seek ministry from your pastor, a Christian counselor, or a trusted friend who can talk and pray with you about such things.

If you desperately want another baby but can't shake your fears about possibly losing another, talk honestly with your doctor about your feelings. Let him comfort you by preparing you mind and heart with *facts.* Don't expect your doctor to be a spiritual or emotional *counselor* to you. Few are either trained or gifted to counsel. Most do not have time for counseling. But they can certainly disarm the anxieties that misinformation causes.

## GOOD GRIEF

Years ago some close friends of ours lost a grandchild. There had been no prior indication that there could be a serious problem. The entire family was emotionally devastated when their little boy was born with an undeveloped brain and with other parts missing or malformed. The baby lived only for a few hours. But during that time the family gave him all they could. His parents loved him. His grandparents held him in the nursery, rocked him, and sang to him. They told him about Jesus.

His uncle talked to him and told him stories about the history of their family. Questions that anyone might have had about the baby's ability to understand were irrelevant. The family was pouring love into the personal spirit of a baby who needed to be claimed and treasured. And when he died, they blessed him and released him to his heavenly Father. Two years later the mother gave birth to a beautiful, healthy baby girl.

Sometimes a mother who has lost a baby, and then conceives another, tries to comfort herself with the thought that she is pregnant again with the child she lost. This can happen when the grieving process has not been completed, and emotional release and healing have not been accomplished. God doesn't "recycle" babies, and if that attitude and expectation prevail, the new baby may always struggle with a deep sense that he or she is a substitute for someone else. Such children may always struggle with rejection and feel as if they can't be loved for who they are.

Every baby is a unique person. Our friend's baby girl is not in any way a replacement for her brother who died. My brother Jerry and his wife were blessed with three fine sons after the loss of their first. But not one is a replacement for the first-born. Not one is like the others. Each is loved and appreciated as a unique gift of God.

What, then, fills the special empty place in the heart of the parents for the one they lost? Nothing but countless expressions of the love of God over a period of time and the believed promise of eternal life and reunion with our loved ones.

## The Trauma of Losing an Older Child

The death of an older child is more difficult to deal with because you have had time to bond more securely. You and your husband have invested years of yourselves and shared countless precious, tender moments with your children. You have played, worked, laughed, and cried together. You have nursed them through the pain of scraped knees and hurt feelings again and again. You have comforted them through failures and celebrated their achievements.

Many important family decisions have been made with top priority given to their well-being. You have been growing in excitement and expectancy concerning each child's capabilities and potential. You have the sense that if your children can become all that they can be, you live! It is not that you live *through* your children's life, but somehow your innermost being is set free to dance, sing, and celebrate in a special, glorious way when you see your sons and daughters flourishing. You rejoice for their sake and for the lives they will touch. Each child's roots are entwined deeply around your heart in such a way that when death uproots him or her, great violence is done to you.

### Understanding and dealing with your husband's response

As I mentioned earlier, your husband cannot truly mourn a miscarriage because the conception has not yet become real to him. He knew you were pregnant, but he has not yet seen, touched, or felt the presence of the child as you have. He has related more to an idea, a hope, and a dream that can be replaced. Your husband may express disappointment, and, if he is sensitive, he may sympathize or even empathize with you. But he can't be expected to feel the loss of one he has never seen or held in the same degree you do.

A man can feel real grief (whether or not he can express it) for the loss of a stillborn baby, especially if he has been participating with his wife in the joy and wonder of the development process. Listening to the heartbeat, placing his hand on her abdomen, and blessing the little one in the womb make the idea of a baby real to him. But he has not yet had the opportunity to bond with the baby as much as his wife has.

When an older child dies, however, your husband goes through the same deep emotional wrenching that you as a mother experience. He too has had time to bond and feel as if a part of himself has been ripped away. He is plagued with feelings of frustration and guilt, as you are: that you were help-less; you couldn't save your loved one from the illness or acci-dent that took his or her life. You are hit again and again with a Niagara of thoughts about what you wish you had said to your child or done for him while he was alive.

If the two of you can share your grief together, console one another, and pray for one another, your relationship will naturally grow stronger. But if either of you is paralyzed by an inability to express emotions or share pain, and withdraws into isolation, the other is left to struggle with overwhelming feelings of rejection and abandonment. A chasm can grow between you that becomes more and more difficult to span.

As I have said before, men in our culture are less equipped to handle the healthy expression of emotion than women. Your husband is the one most likely to withdraw. Understand what is really happening. Do not allow yourself to perceive his standoffish reaction as personal rejection and abandonment. Insofar as you are able, with God helping you, here are a few tips to keep in mind:

- Do not react in the same manner. Two people withdrawing only widen the chasm.

- Do not accuse him of being insensitive or try to manipulate him.

- For your own sake (you are vulnerable), find a "safe" friend or counselor with whom to talk and pray.

- Pray for your husband to have strength of spirit to let his emotions live, to open his heart and let you in, and to talk with you.

- Pray that the Lord will supply your need and bring every message of demand in you to death.

- Touch your husband with gentle, sensitive affection as often as he will allow.

- If he pushes you away, understand that he does so out of fear of losing control. Back off, pray silently for him, and try again later. Pray that your touch will be a comfort, a blessing, and an *invitation.*

When you are tempted to say to him, "Don't you know…?" "Can't you see…?" or "Why can't you…?"—zip your lips, and say something more along the lines of, "You're hurting, aren't you? I understand." Sensitive, loving, affirmative persistence is a powerfully effective (though not guaranteed) bridge to span chasms created by grief, hurt, and fear.

The kind of discipline I have described is not easy when your own heart is bleeding. You can't keep from feeling that your husband is supposed to be the priest of the house. He should be concerned for you and taking some kind of initiative toward you. It doesn't seem fair. Why should you have to be the "strong" one?

It is natural for you to feel as you do, but if you hold on to those feelings and feed them or wallow in them, you may fall into dark depths of depression that fill the chasm between you. It is far more difficult to rise from that. God will empower your attempts to forgive, heal, bless, and confront in love. He will not empower your choices to hold on to anger, bitterness, self-pity, or accusation, or to wield them as weapons of aggression or defense.

### Understanding your own responses

Suppose you find yourself crying incessantly and uncontrollably in the grieving process. You can't understand what is the matter with you. You are trying to relate to your husband in a sensitive and loving way, but it seems impossible when *you* are a total mess of emotions. The more emotional you become, the further he flees from you. You feel strange, alien even to yourself, and you begin to fear that you could be headed toward a nervous breakdown.

There are at least two powerful dynamics at work here. In chapter two, I spoke of the way in which a wife unconsciously identifies with her husband because of their one-flesh relationship. This is the first dynamic. She experiences the feelings he cannot express, carries the burdens he has not talked about, and cries the tears he cannot cry. When parents have lost a child and the father withdraws into isolation, tightly bound by intense, ungrieved grief, and fears sharing with anyone, his wife may carry the load and cry for both of them.

The second dynamic in operation is what my husband, John, and I call the "balance principle." If one partner is extremely talkative, the other becomes quiet. If one fails to discipline the children, the other tends to over-discipline. If one seems foolishly adventurous, the other develops a cautious attitude that appears to be cowardice.

We were created to complement, uplift, and strengthen one another in our differences. But when significant areas of our personality have not yet been surrendered to God and redeemed, we are too much controlled by old habitual practices in our nature. Then instead of blessing and fulfilling each other, we drive one another to extremes.

If a husband cannot express his hurt and grief openly, his wife will probably go to the other extreme with the combined weight and power of the grief in both of them. She can't understand why she has become so emotional and nearly out of control, but it is only that she is counterbalancing her husband and bearing his ungrieved grief.

If this is what is happening to you, what can you do? Recognize the dynamics at work. Quit worrying about your sanity. Tell the Lord about it. Lift and relinquish *all* the load to Him, and go about your business. Repeat. Repeat. Repeat...until it is no longer a problem.

There are consecutive stages of grief connected with any loss: denial, anger, guilt, depression, acceptance, and then healing. We need to know that God loves us as we move through that natural sequence in the gift of His grace.

### Learning to accept that a child is gone

So where is the final consolation in relation to a child who dies? How do you learn to accept that a child is no longer a part of life? The answer is found in the child's life and legacy.

There is a story in the Bible that says it all:

> And they were bringing children to Him so that He might touch them; and the disciples rebuked them. But when Jesus saw this, He was indignant and said to them, "*Permit the children to come to Me; do not hinder them; for the kingdom of God belongs to such as these. Truly I say to you, whoever does not receive the kingdom of God like a child shall not enter it at all." And He took them in His arms and began blessing them, laying His hands upon them.*
> —MARK 10:13–16, *emphasis added*

My little cousin Charlie was one of God's special gifts. He was a beautiful boy with an outstanding, keen intellect, a bright, happy nature, and a zest for living that inspired all the family. I remember vividly his soft, blond, curly hair and blue eyes, delightfully entertaining chatter, sense of humor, and enthusiastic hugs.

He loved the stories the family read to him and had memorized most of them word for word. He loved to sing and could carry a tune very well. His favorite songs were the ones he learned at Sunday school. When he sang, "Jesus loves me, this I know," we were certain he knew from the depths of his heart the truth of what he was singing.

Before Charlie started kindergarten, he went into the hospital for what everyone thought would be a simple tonsillectomy. Something went wrong. We never knew just what it was. Someone guessed it might have been an allergy to the anesthetic.

Little Charlie died. But before he died, he left a beautiful gift for us to remember—a gift that exemplified the blessing his short life had been. His parents went in to see him as he was coming out of the anesthetic, and he said to them, "I'm sorry I can't sing for you today."

Little Charlie left behind a beautiful memory of what it means to have childlike faith. And we know that today he is singing for the Father from the depths of his heart.

## FROM THE GUILT OF ABORTION TO FORGIVENESS AND FREEDOM

Though most of our children came as surprises, and none of them at "convenient" times, I fought with everything within me not to lose them. The cold, hard logic of the world would have said we couldn't afford them, but somehow overwhelming love rose up from within John and me to welcome and embrace each one.

By God's grace we've managed to get through college and seminary; feed, clothe, and educate the kids; pay our bills; and enjoy a rich, stimulating, challenging, fulfilling, and fun-filled family life and ministry all along the way. Praise God for the quiver full of arrows He gave us!

We live in a crazy, mixed-up, sinful world where the murdering of millions of babies in wombs of mothers who *could* provide for their offspring, but choose not to, takes place each year. Some of these women act in fear and panic, unable to believe they have any alternative, and they may grieve deeply.

Others dehumanize the children they have killed as a convenience in order to rationalize their actions and deny their guilt. What they don't realize is that while "fetus" may *sound* more like a "thing" than a "person," it is really only the Latin word for "baby." Though many women feel relieved initially after an abortion, suppressed guilt and ungrieved grief eventually take a tremendous toll in illness or nervous disorders, and these women find themselves in desperate need of healing.

If you are one of these women, I want you to know that healing is available for you. Receiving forgiveness is a natural consequence of repentance for sin. And forgiveness lays the groundwork for healing that God *longs* to bring. *But repentance is the key*. Repentance for:

- Giving in to someone else's pressure to get rid of an unwanted child.

- Accepting the lie that it was OK, that you were justified by your unique circumstances.

- Not wanting to be bothered.

- Choosing material comforts rather than the life of the baby, your own flesh.

- Being afraid of the responsibility of raising a child, or of being too young.

- Hiding the embarrassment of illegitimacy.

- Whatever you thought your reasons were— repentance for *murdering* your child.

I know it sounds so harsh to put it that way, but until you repent of the abortion as a murder, you will never be free. Guilt is your friend. You can't receive forgiveness until you admit your guilt. Guilt is not the same thing as condemnation.

Murder is not the unforgivable sin. Rationalization will hold you forever in bondage to the stresses of hidden guilt and the compulsive need for self-defense. To know you are forgiven is to be truly free to get on with your life.

Over the years John and I counseled many women who were weighed down with the guilt of a past abortion. Normally we don't push people to have an emotional experience. But in the case of abortion, since we know that they had to "dehumanize" their baby in order to kill him or her, they need now to give themselves permission to experience some real emotions about the death of their child. For too long they have lived in that practice of denying reality. If you are in this position, here is what we suggest:

- Ask yourself (or ask God to let you know) if the baby would have been a boy or a girl.

- What might you have named the baby?

- What might this child have looked like?

- What might the child have accomplished in his/her life?

As women have pondered these questions, some have discovered surprising and heart-wrenching reality in dreams, in visions, or in "just knowing." And almost all have broken through to sob in grief for their lost child. "For the sorrow that is according to the will of God produces a repentance without regret, leading to salvation; but the sorrow of the world produces death" (2 Cor. 7:10). With the deep sobbing have come cleansing and healing—and with forgiveness, the beginning of restored health and self-esteem.

*Chapter 6*

# MIXED SIGNALS— LEARNING *to* HANDLE EMOTIONAL OVERLOAD

S I WAS TYPING this book, my computer locked up because I gave it too many signals at the same time, and it had the good sense not to try to respond to them all at once. It simply refused to do anything until I turned it off for a moment and started it again with one signal at a time. I have often wished the computers of our inner beings were as quick to stop in response to overload and as obedient to proper new directions following a time of rest and reflection.

If we persist in overloading our mental, emotional, or spiritual circuits without taking sufficient time to sort out, prioritize, digest, and pray, we run into confusion. And then, if we plunge ahead to press the "print" button, the garbled messages we project fail miserably to communicate in a redemptive way what is in our hearts.

Even an overload of positive or valuable information can have a negative effect on a person's emotions. Years ago someone spoke to me following a conference where John and I had taught what we considered to be simple basics of biblical counseling. "This was absolutely wonderful! Beyond my expectations! But it's the first time I feel like I've been fed with a fire hose!" he said.

"How does it make you feel?" I asked. "Like you need to burp?"

"I don't really know. I guess I'm afraid I won't be able to remember it all."

"Don't try. Go home and do something absolutely earthy, something fun and relaxing. Everything will fall into place, and you'll find yourself remembering when you need it. No cause for sweat. If it's important, God will bring it up and run it by again."

"OK!" he replied.

The word I gave to that person was received as welcome relief. The admonition to relax and let everything settle met no resistance because his anxiety feelings had only been in reaction to too many positive signals. But when negative signals have come with the force of a fire hose, the recipient finds it extremely difficult to embrace any kind of a "let it go for now" message.

Letting go of your feelings sounds like an invitation to irresponsibility or insanity and destruction, but it really isn't.

## CONCERNING THE NATURE
## AND PLACE OF FEELINGS

For most people, feelings often falsely represent objective reality. They don't understand that our personal feelings have to do *only* with our *subjective* experiences, interpretations, and responses. Our experiences are limited, our interpretations colored, and our responses greatly influenced by what has already lodged in our hearts—from an accumulation of current unhealed, unreleased stresses, or perhaps even from our earliest childhood experiences.

Any number of things can easily affect our feelings—what we have eaten, how well we have slept, what time of the month it is, whether the man in our life has recently and sincerely kissed us, how many times the phone has rung while we have been trying to prepare dinner, and the list goes on.

As a woman, when you have come under a tyranny of negative feelings and someone tells you to focus on something else for a little while until your emotions have settled or you've "calmed down," it makes you feel angry and rejected, doesn't it? You feel as if the person doesn't understand the problem or doesn't accept you. The person has "questioned the validity" of your perceptions. You perceive it as lack of respect for the way you feel, and it hurts you even more.

Because you have exalted your personal feelings as *truth*, you defend and nurse your feelings, and therefore these feelings easily take you captive. When someone suggests a need to relax, that a situation might not warrant such intensity, you often feel accused. How often have you said or heard someone say:

- "What? You don't think I ought to feel upset?!"

- "Wouldn't you be upset if that had happened to you?"

- "You're saying there is something wrong with me!"

You have only two alternatives: you can hide or deny your feelings, plus suppress them and wallow in them, or you can exalt your feelings, insist, persist—and wallow! More often than not, we women usually do the latter. But even if you choose denial, it is only a matter of time before the pressure of what has been suppressed increases to the point of an eruption. The wallowing time is what has increased the force of the explosion, whereas had you not believed and nurtured your feelings, time would have brought balance and rest.

Few who exalt their feelings can successfully shut them down, but those who are successful in turning off their emotions most often also lose the capacity to feel the positive emotions that enable a person to experience zest for life. You can spiral into depression from either direction.

## LET YOUR FEELINGS LIVE!

Everyone has feelings. *The important thing is what we learn to do with them.* We should allow our feelings to live. Even though they often fail to represent objective truth, they are good indicators of what has lodged in our hearts. But we are in trouble if our minds make decisions solely based upon what we are feeling. Our hearts' emotions were not intended to rule our minds and direct our actions.

> For from *within*, out of the *heart* of men, proceed the evil thoughts, fornications, thefts, murders, adulteries, deeds of coveting and wickedness, as well as deceit, sensuality, envy, slander, pride and foolishness. All these evil things proceed from *within* and defile the man.
> —MARK 7:21–23, *emphasis added*

In other words, we are to be *renewed* in the spirit of our *minds* (Eph. 4:23). With the renewed mind we may instruct our heart in what to do with the emotions we feel, how to act, and how to "put on the new self, created to be like God in *true* righteousness and holiness" (Eph. 4:24, NIV, emphasis added).

John and I had taught these principles for years, thinking we understood what we were saying. But what we had known with our minds is now much better known with our hearts.

## FEELINGS WILL TEST YOUR FOUNDATION

There are seasons in our lives when feelings arise and try the foundation of our lives until we think we will burst. How we react and handle our emotions during such a season is a test of our mettle, if you will. It shows us for who we truly are.

Luke 6:48 says:

> He is like a man building a house, who dug deep and laid a foundation upon the rock; and when a flood rose, the torrent burst against that house and could not shake it, because it had been well built.

Years ago John and I came home from an intense traveling and teaching schedule hoping to find rest, only to be hit with a series of the most stressful and emotionally disturbing situations we have ever had to face. First, we discovered a family crisis that nearly shattered the lives of our family members and us, physically and emotionally.

John and I discovered we were capable of powerful feelings we had never known before. We had always been able to identify empathetically with counselees in the counseling process. But it was somewhat devastating and certainly humbling to realize that we could hate as deeply as we loved, and that we could even want to kill!

It took an unbelievable amount of grace and discipline in prayer, as well as every ounce of energy we had, to make the requisite choices to forgive (Matt. 6:14–15), not just once but again and again over an extended period of time as things got worse and worse. It stretched our faith tremendously to continue to make ourselves believe that the Lord could bring good out of such as a mess as this. Though His work is not yet completed, He is faithfully, bit by bit, turning ashes into garlands in the life of each one involved. We are tremendously thankful.

While this was going on, we had to dismiss a staff member of the ministry for not repenting of the sins in his own life. A few in the local community, not understanding the circumstances, turned against us for that. We struggled with more feelings and had to make aggressive choices to forgive.

At the same time, healing ministries were coming under attack through literature. Our ministry, as well as others, was grossly misrepresented and misquoted. Disappointingly, far too many readers did not possess sufficient information to challenge these errors or discern what was happening. The sales of our books dropped from best-selling books to one-third of their former sales. We also found out that we were owed thousands of dollars in royalty payments, but were denied the money. More feelings; more choices. More hours of prayer on bended knees.

But the feelings with which we had to struggle the most were hurts and griefs for the many people who had now become afraid to reach out for help anywhere for fear of getting into something they had been led to believe might be erroneous or even occultic.

We were disillusioned to find again and again that most of the Christians who objected to our (and others') teachings were reacting on the basis of hearsay—they had never even read or heard firsthand the material they were reviling and rejecting! We grieved also because of the division that was aggravated in the body of Christ.

## WHERE WAS GOD?

Admittedly, like the psalmists, we wondered from time to time where the Lord was while all this was going on. We had been walking His walk as best we knew how. We had no lack of testimonies concerning miracles of healing the Lord had accomplished throughout our ministry. Was He tending His flock? Though mentally we knew the answer very well, we found ourselves straining at emotional levels.

God reminded us that He hadn't promised to keep us out of all difficulty and that He would take care of His wounded children and torn body. Scripture says there will be various trials. What God did promise was that He would be with us *in* trouble (Ps. 91:15). In our listening during our devotional times, the Lord also said to us that because of free will, He cannot and will not prevent anyone from sinning. But He will hold each one accountable.

We spent a lot of time in prayer, acknowledging our feelings each time they surfaced, giving them (raw and unpolished) to the Lord. (He is big enough to hear honest confessions without falling off His throne.)

We kept asking His forgiveness for our anger and resentment, telling Him we didn't know how to accomplish forgiveness toward others, but we were willing to make the choices anyhow and would trust Him to make our choices real.

Obediently, we prayed blessing for our enemies. God was faithful then, and He is faithful now. He is blessing us beyond our expectations. Satan has not stolen our joy in the Lord, nor has he prevented Jesus' redemptive process.

## THE EMOTIONAL BATTLE BETWEEN THE SEXES

Everyone has feelings, but how women handle their feelings greatly differs from how men handle them.

During this stressful time for John and me, I learned something about the difference between men's and women's emotions. I had always wondered why so many men seem to be detached emotionally in times of crisis.

Sometimes I would hurt so badly I could almost hear my insides screaming. And as I prayed in intercession, I would occasionally feel physical pain, as if I were in the last stages of childbirth. But even giving birth to six children had far less cumulative pain than what we were presently enduring.

Each time another detail of the one-after-another blows would hit, I would feel a new wave of pain and nausea, and I would weep, at least on the inside. John, on the other hand, seemed most often to stiffen up and withdraw. At least on the surface, John sometimes appeared to be hard and uncaring. But I knew he was every bit as sensitive and caring as I.

Nevertheless, while I wanted him to be as solid *as* a rock, I didn't want him to *be* one. I wanted him to cry with me, but he couldn't or wouldn't. I couldn't understand why. When I tried to talk to him concerning my feelings, my efforts seemed only to drive him more deeply behind the walls of his private retreat or into the oblivion of the television.

"John, I'm sorry I don't have a 'right' way to express myself. I'm just hurting. I can't 'find' you, and we need to stand together."

Silence.

"John, where are you? What are you doing in there all by yourself?"

"I'm just thinking."

"What are you thinking?"

"I don't know. I'm not ready to talk about it yet."

"I wish you could present your thoughts unpolished. Share the process with me."

Silence.

I knew that to press John further would be like beating on a deep bruise. So I described my feelings to the Lord and understood that I could not expect John, who was every bit as wounded as I, to do for me what only God could do. I prayed comfort and strength of spirit for my husband and saturated myself with the Word of God, which is infinitely substantial and true:

> I sought the LORD, and *He* answered me, and delivered me from all my fears.
> —PSALM 34:4, *emphasis added*

> Do not fret because of evildoers…for they will wither quickly like the grass….Trust in the LORD, and do good…and *He* will give you the desires of your heart. Commit your way to the LORD, trust also in *Him*…and *He* will bring forth your righteousness as the light, and your judgment as the noonday. Rest in the LORD and wait patiently for *Him*; do not fret because of him who prospers in his way….Cease from anger, and forsake wrath.
> —PSALM 37:1–8, *emphasis added*

I talked to myself:

> Why are you in despair, O my soul? And why have you become disturbed within me? *Hope in God, for I shall again praise Him for the help of His presence.*
> —PSALM 42:5, *emphasis added*

At first I was just going through the motions—choosing and persisting in a discipline because I knew I had to. In the process God made His presence real to me. I know that John, in his own way, was doing likewise.

Our family member, in the intensity and confusion of her shattered life, had to do the same thing. She was able to share some feelings with loved ones who listened and supported and prayed for her. But no one but God could reach the innermost core of the terrible hurt, pain, insecurity, loneliness, and anxiety that threatened for a while to drag her into craziness.

Despite her feelings, she struggled to persist in a discipline of choosing to do what she knew would put her in a place of receiving from the Lord. Even while inner emotional foundations seemed to be slipping, and her world was falling down around her, she continued to attend church. She attended a cell group, taught a Sunday school class, read the Word, and prayed. In the process, Father God showed up with gifts of strength to stand, grace to forgive, loving-kindness to enable repentance, and real redemptive power.

The question remained: Why could we, as women, verbalize feelings so much more easily than John? Why does this difference between men and women manifest so consistently to cause hurtful misunderstandings and frustration?

I learned the answer to the emotional difference between the sexes years ago when I listened to an enlightening interview conducted by Dr. James Dobson with Dr. Donald Joy, who reported concerning some research being done on the right and left brain in males and females.[1] The research suggested that men use the left hemisphere of their brain (which is the logical, analytical side), while women tend to use mainly the right hemisphere of their brain (which is the creative, emotional side).

As women, we can feel so alone when that important underlying part of our emotional makeup is missed!

## BEING MULTITASK-ORIENTED VERSUS HAVING A ONE-TRACK MIND

I remember well the years when our six children were growing up and I was a busy pastor's wife. The doorbell and the telephone were almost continually in competition with the children for my attention. I never knew when someone's crisis would arrive on our doorstep, or when our dinner would need to be stretched to feed someone who was hungry for food and tender loving care.

Our backyard was always full of the neighbors' children, to the extent that we laughingly (most of the time) threatened to put up a sign saying, "Public Playground—Everybody Welcome." I always had to be ready for a spontaneous invasion of little people who forever needed to get a drink or to use "the potty." Teenagers from the church frequently dropped by after school and stayed to talk awhile.

Prayer meetings and youth group meetings were usually held in our home, largely because we couldn't afford to have a babysitter. Sunday looked nothing like a day of rest for us, and at times we had not yet learned to say "no" to those who called on Monday to plead, "I know this is your day off, but I'm dying." "Free time" was not even a part of my vocabulary.

Sometimes John would come home, recognize a quality of frazzledness in my countenance, and say, "Honey, you look tired. Maybe we could go out to eat this evening." Being the practical and thrifty person that I am, I would respond, "That would be great, John, but we really can't afford it."

What I was really saying was that I was glad he noticed how tired I was and, although I was aware of the limitations of our budget, that I desperately hoped he would have more regard for me than the budget. (McDonald's would do!) I *wanted* him to press beyond my protest to persuade me to receive the blessing of his gift because he loved me.

One time John asked me, "Why don't you just say what you mean?"

I replied, "Because you're supposed to know!"

He was mystified. It was difficult for him to understand why my having to tell him what I wanted could spoil the blessing of his giving. I was supposed to know that he loved me whether he thought to tell me or not!

We have each had to recognize many habits of thinking and feeling in "*supposed to*" terms, die to our demands, and believe that we are chosen and cherished by the other despite our dissimilarities in perceptions and responses. I had to learn not to take his "hard" logic personally, which occasionally seemed to disrespect and offend my sensitivities.

Over the years I have grown to appreciate John's ability to help me sort and order my sometimes overwhelming flood of feelings with his peculiarly male thought patterns. And he, in turn, has learned to receive with respect my perceptions that, though usually accurate, sometimes lack a conscious and explainable premise.

Because I am a woman, I could simultaneously cook dinner, talk on the telephone, hug one child as he came past me in the kitchen, and still be aware of the baby who had headed toward the open door to the stairway. My beloved "left-brained" husband usually focuses on one thing at a time.

It is, in one sense, a blessing that he can completely tune out noise and motion to read, pray, write, and create with rapt concentration. But if I had not been nearby to receive and attend to the multitude of signals he had tuned out, our family would possibly have been in trouble.

I used to be quite perturbed with John when he would become so totally occupied with what he was doing that he failed to hear or see what our children were doing. I thought he was being negligent because of a warped or underdeveloped sense of priority. When our oldest son, Loren, was one year old, he lavishly decorated our entire living room floor with talcum powder while his father sat in the same room, reading. Coming back into our apartment, I fairly shrieked, "John—how *could* you not see what he was doing?!"

Now, as grandparents, we are older and wiser. When John watches the little grandchildren, that is exactly what he does— he *watches* the grandchildren.

## THE PROBLEM OF SMALL TALK

Women often talk with one another about what everyone already knows, and if it doesn't go on endlessly, we will enjoy the conversation. Men can't understand that at all. They may even feel insulted if a woman persists in delivering to them information that, to their way of thinking, contains nothing new or edifying. It sounds to them like a waste of time. Or like endless repetition of stories bordering on gossip. They may say so and seriously wound the sensitivities of the women they care about.

Many men tend to be bored and impatient with embellishments that seem not to be central to issues. Most of the time they don't understand that we communicate far more than verbal messages when we talk. We may be only venting stress. But more often we are tuning in to one another beneath the messages, sharing nuances of feeling and forming emotional bridges and parameters for relationships.

Words spoken may merely be vehicles for what is actually being given or received from heart to heart and spirit to spirit. I am not at all sure that we are consciously aware of this dynamic. We simply do what we do. But I am certain that we are often deeply wounded when men we care about seem to belittle or ridicule us—even when it is only by humorously or affectionately flavored comments. Understanding that men function in a different emotional way than females do, and that many aspects of us are a mystery to them, should help us not to receive every negative-sounding comment as personal criticism and rejection.

God has designed and equipped men and women not to battle but to appreciate, bless, and balance one another with our differences. How do we do that? We must walk in a discipline:

> 1. *Recognize our basic differences without putting any value judgment on them.* God knew what He was doing when He made us the way He did.

> 2. *Die to our demands that another person must think and feel like we do.* If men and women were alike, it might be comfortable, but it would certainly be boring. And we would lose the value of the balance principle.

> 3. *Choose to forgive when others treat us insensitively.* Isn't that what women want from men? Eventually we get what we give (Matt. 6:14–15; Gal. 6:7; Matt. 7:1–2). Know that we can't make forgiveness happen. That is God's task. Our job is to make the choice again and again. Unforgiveness held in the heart is a poison that will defile others and eventually destroy us. It is also a force that warps our

perspective and prevents us from recognizing the other person's attempts to change for the better. And it is a seed sown that will cause us to reap in kind.

4. *Tell God immediately how we feel about an injury or slight.* Do this in a "flash prayer" before the emotion has a chance to lodge in our hearts. He is big enough to handle the full force of our initial uncensored, unsorted, unpolished emotions. Our spouses, children, friends, and associates probably are not.

You may protest, "But I'm not a Christian! I'm not even sure I believe God is real. Or—if He is—why should He listen to me?"

Try this consistently over a period of time anyway, and see what a difference it makes!

5. *Ask God to speak His best response through us.* This may be silence. It may be a soft word. It may be a stern word. It may be an apology, an explanation, or a confrontation. It may even be a choice to spend time apart from the other person for a time.

The important thing is, if we submit our fleshly response to God without defending our self-righteousness, He then has an opportunity to express a redemptive word or deed through us that, by His Spirit, can possibly contribute to healing and reconciliation, and to the building of relationship.

If you continue to struggle unsuccessfully in the same areas, something deeper may be necessary. You would be wise to talk and pray with a Christian counselor concerning the possible *root* causes for the fruit produced repeatedly in your life:

For there is no good tree which produces bad fruit.
—LUKE 6:43

You may have experienced wounds during your foundational years (before you were six), from which fear, resentment, and bitterness have been stored in your heart. These may hold you in bondage, shaping and fueling your present responses to hurt. They may perpetuate childish ways of thinking, feeling, and doing, thus keeping you from making decisions you want to make and acting on them.

## STANDING ON SHAKY GROUND

"Hi, Mary, what's for supper?" George says as he comes through the door and sinks into his favorite chair to watch TV.

"How was your day, George?" Mary replies. He doesn't answer. *He didn't even kiss me when he came in the door; that would've been nice, but he's tired. That's OK. He'll feel better after dinner.* Mary issues a call to their four enthusiastically hungry children playing in the backyard, "Kids, come inside and wash your hands...dinner's ready! George, dinner's ready!"

Scurrying through the back door, the youngest falls down, trampled under the mob of his older siblings.

"Are you OK, baby?" Mary comforts him and kisses him on the head. "Kids, please watch out for George Jr.!"

As the children rush again, this time to reach the table, little Joe manages to spill a glass of milk onto the floor.

"Joe, I've told you a thousand times, please slow down. Everyone is going to have a chance to eat—including you. Now where's your dad?" As Mary mops the mess, she bellows again, "George, dinner's ready!"

"OK—just a minute," George bellows back.

"George, everyone is ready. Didn't you hear me call you?"

"I'll be there in a minute. They're on the five-yard line."

"George, the children are hungry. We're all sitting at the table, and the food is getting cold. Will you *please* come—now?!"

"*I said* I'll be there in minute!"

Minutes pass.

"George, are you coming? Shall we go ahead and eat without you?"

"Mary, get off my back! I'm tired, and I don't need that yackety-yak."

By this time, Mary is being hit with all kinds of emotional signals:

    &#8477;   *Does he think he's the only one who has worked all day? I'd like to get lost once in a while in the TV, but who'd watch the kids?*

    &#8477;   *I called him in plenty of time. The kids heard me from the backyard. Is he deaf?*

    &#8477;   *Why should I fix a good, hot meal only to let it sit there and get cold because he has to watch one more play? They'll rerun it on the late news anyway.*

    &#8477;   *Doesn't he know what kind of example he's setting for his children?*

    &#8477;   *Doesn't he know what that communicates to the kids? How important are they anyway? What happened to priorities?*

   &#8765;   *Why did he have to snap at me like that in front of the children?*

With all the steam from her inner boiling point of judgment, unforgiveness, and bitterness lodged in her heart, Mary overreacts and angrily shouts back, "Why do you always have to come late to the dinner table?"

For the moment Mary is so overcome by her own feelings that she can't discern the situation or control her emotions.

What is Mary—or George, for that matter—to do?

This is a fictitious story, but it is one that probably any person could substitute his or her name for Mary's or George's.

## JESUS HAS ALREADY DONE IT FOR YOU!

The example of how Mary's signals triggered her reaction is the key to showing us something greater. That is, basic attitudes and feelings that become compulsive are formed from fractures that occur in our emotional and spiritual foundations. The bad news is that long-term pressures on such foundations cause our house to crumble. If Mary doesn't learn to deal with the underlying issues, they could eventually cause severe problems in her marriage and family life. The good news is that Jesus Christ is able to re-lay, and renew, our foundations if we allow Him.

In Luke 6, Jesus spoke a message to His disciples. He speaks of evil coming out of the *treasure of the heart*: "his [the evil man's] mouth speaks from that which fills his heart" (Luke 6:45). Then He goes on to chide His disciples for calling Him, "Lord, Lord," without the willingness to *dig deep* to lay a *foundation* upon the rock for a house that will stand in the midst of a torrential flood (vv. 46–49).

Many Christians celebrate that they are new creatures and resist the idea that they now have anything within the heart to deal with. Yet they struggle and often fail to live the life and faith they profess. The Word of God is clear:

> Our old self was crucified with Him, *that our body of sin might be done away with*, that we should no longer be slaves to sin; for he who has died is freed from sin.
> —Romans 6:6–7, *emphasis added*

What Paul is saying here is that "our body of sin" (not our sinful body) is made up not only of the recognizably sinful thoughts and deeds we have committed, but also of *all* the old habits and practices we built before we became new creatures. We may be "new creatures," but all we have known is based upon what we have already experienced in life. Just as a baby learns first to crawl before he walks, we need to practice new motives and modes of operating.

At times we may be frustrated, but it is the only way we know how to reach our goal. Sometimes we try to run ahead, and we end up falling on our faces, which leaves us emotionally traumatized, even if for a moment. So we revert to a way that is the most comfortable for us, one that makes us feel as if we're in control. The point is to take small steps so that we gain strength and confidence until we can run the race with endurance.

The apostle Paul knew that he had to grow and mature into the fullness of who he was:

> Not that I have already obtained it [resurrection life], or have already become perfect, but I press on in order that I may lay hold of that for which also I was laid hold of by Jesus Christ.
>
> —Philippians 3:12

He lived and encouraged us all to live in a discipline of saying "no" to the old, familiar, and seductive ways, and to offer ourselves to the Lord for the power to make a new choice.

> Even so consider ["reckon" in KJV] yourselves to be dead to sin, but alive to God in Christ Jesus. Therefore *do not let sin reign* in your mortal body that you should obey its lusts, and *do not go on presenting the members of your body to sin* as instruments of unrighteousness; but *present yourselves to God* as those alive from the dead, and your members as instruments of righteousness to God.
> —ROMANS 6:11–13, *emphasis added*

Such a discipline is necessarily a daily business. Paul said, "I die *daily*" (1 Cor. 15:31, emphasis added).

> I *have been crucified* with Christ; and it is no longer I who live, but Christ lives in me; and the life which I now live in the flesh I live by faith in the Son of God, who loved me, and delivered Himself up for me.
> —GALATIANS 2:20, *emphasis added*

What emotional balance and rest we can enjoy when we have acknowledged, confessed, and crucified the driving signals of bitterness from the past!

*Chapter 7*

# COPING WITH
# *a* LOVED ONE'S
# SUBSTANCE ABUSE

I F YOU HAVE A spouse or child who is addicted to drugs or alcohol, you know the pain of total devastation, not only personally, but also because such abuse touches the *entire* family. You've run the gamut of emotions—hurt, disillusionment, anger, blame, loss, loneliness—and you haven't any idea about where to turn or what to do.

Although I personally don't know what it's like to live with a husband or children who abuse substances (and I thank God for it!), John and I have many years of counseling experience and have ministered to people in this area. In this chapter, I will share with you the stories of two people whom we counseled, followed by what I pray will be helpful tips as you walk through this valley.

## LIVING WITH AN ALCOHOLIC HUSBAND

Ken and Donna Campbell have been an integral part of our personal (and corporate) life for quite some time, and we are very grateful to God for that. John and I have walked with them through some of the deepest and darkest moments in their lives. Today they are a beautiful couple who minister to others, but it was not always so.

Ken and Donna's marriage did not get off to a good start. While he was away at college, she lived with her parents, and Donna and Ken had only the weekends together. She came from a loving home where affection was expressed, but he grew up in a family where emotions and affection were reserved. He had a difficult time showing emotions and rarely shared his feelings with anyone.

As a child, Donna had been molested, which caused her to have a poor self-image and low self-esteem. Later, when she met Ken, he was gentle and shy, which made her feel safe, but after their marriage, she felt inhibited sexually because of her childhood experience, which caused her to be unhappy and to have marital problems.

After Ken graduated from college, they made their home apart from Donna's parents. But he was working as a traveling salesman, frequently making overnight trips, leaving her feeling lonely and insecure.

Both poured themselves into their jobs, kept late hours, and were overtired when they did have time to spend together. Weekends were spent doing chores—cleaning house and doing laundry. There was no real sharing, no fun, and their communication was seriously breaking down.

Donna allowed herself to become vulnerable, which ultimately led to an affair.

When Ken first learned of her infidelity, he was crushed. His first thought was to divorce her, but then he chose to stay and work things out. As much as they tried, their efforts were superficial. They did not understand how deep the roots of fear and insecurity at the heart level were that were pulling them apart.

They moved several times while he continued working as a salesman. Ken was given an expense account and was told to "socialize"—to become involved in men's clubs in order to foster accounts.

They eventually moved back to their hometown, where Ken accepted a position as manager of a savings and loan company. Now he was *required* to belong to every social club he could in order to make a name in the community. He worked hard at his job and made a great success of it. But in the process, the "thing to do" was to take the guys—associates and clients—out to a bar to talk awhile. Soon it became more than socialization. Ken began to reward himself at the end of the workday by stopping at a bar to relax. As time went on, the stops became more frequent, and he became addicted to alcohol.

By the time their third child was born, Ken was doing a *lot* of drinking. It left Donna feeling angry, abandoned, and betrayed. She was so resentful that she hated him; she didn't even want Ken to touch her.

Donna's emotions and married life were spiraling out of control and began affecting her health. But, providentially, there came a new beginning. (It was during this time in their lives that we met them.)

Ken was drinking even more heavily, and Donna spent countless hours looking out the window, waiting for him to come home.

"Why is he drinking, spending money?" she would ask. Her mind raced with thoughts such as: *Who is he with? He's*

*not interested in me anymore. There must be someone he likes
better than me. Why am I here? What am I good for? If I left,
how could I support four kids?*

As their pastors, John and I each ministered to Ken and
Donna alone; sometimes we also ministered as a couple.
John became like the father they never had, and after Donna's
mom passed away, I became a mother figure to her.

When a person's spouse turns to alcohol or drugs, the
person experiences emotional woundedness, similar to the
woundedness felt if the spouse had an affair. She might feel
lonely, replaced, violated, and angry, as in Donna's case. So
when a caregiver of the opposite sex comes along and offers
help, comfort, strength, understanding, and parental-type
affection, it is natural for the wounded person to experience a
transfer of affection to the caregiver. As their counselors and
pastors, John and I were careful to establish boundaries within
the counselor/counselee role and maintain the integrity of the
relationship, while continuing to offer our love, support, and
prayers.

Ken had left the banking business to go into real estate;
he owned two offices and was doing very well when disaster
hit the Silver Valley in North Idaho. A large corporation had
purchased a local silver, lead, and zinc mine and smelter, but
then bled the company's finances and closed it down. The
economy of the area plummeted radically, and real estate
could scarcely be given away. Ken struggled as long as he could,
finally lost his business, and was forced to declare bankruptcy.
He was devastated and humiliated.

He pummeled himself emotionally again and again: "Why
didn't Donna leave me years ago?" Ken began crying out to
God sincerely from the bottom of the black hole he was in.
They lost everything.

I spent a lot of time with Donna, letting her cry on my shoulder and praying with her for Ken's condition. I also helped her recognize her abilities, her natural beauty, and her value as a wife and mother. She also came to realize that Ken had abilities she could admire.

Our two families became very close, and Ken and Donna could see that we loved them. We gently, but firmly, warned him about the blessings that he was throwing away when he drank. We were careful to hold him accountable without crucifying him. We never ceased praying that the Lord would set him free.

Shortly thereafter, things came to a head. Ken was brought home by the police at five o'clock one morning. He had been given a DUI citation; his driver's license was severely restricted so that he wasn't allowed to drive at night. Ken had to serve a weekend in jail, and God did something during that time: Donna and Ken's relationship started to change, and they began to talk and share again.

Then suddenly, Ken suffered a major heart attack. That was the last stage of the breaking he had to go through. While he was in intensive care for six weeks, Donna realized how much she really loved him. She began to see their relationship from a totally different perspective. She prayed earnestly, "Lord, spare his life. You surely have something much better planned for our lives than we have known or seen."

God not only healed Ken's heart physically, but emotionally and spiritually as well. His drinking (and smoking several packs a day) stopped without a single withdrawal problem.

Despite all of Donna's anger and frustration, she knew she could not afford to nurse any kind of resentment even for a moment.

Yes, it hurts to forgive, but God can endow you with divine power to cope. You can choose to forgive, but you can't change anybody. That is the Lord's job. The enemy wants you, as a believer, to focus on the guilt and shame of the past. Once you have repented of your past sins and forgiven those who have hurt you, focus instead on the redemptive power of the Lord.

Ken and Donna both realized that, when John and I ministered to them, it was by the Lord's leading and with His care and love. The Lord placed us in each other's lives and has built a foundation of deep love and friendship that will last forever.

In essence, that is what the body of Christ is all about.

## ANNA'S STORY—LIVING WITH AN ALCOHOLIC PARENT

(Anna's name has been changed at her request. I recount her story as she told it to me.)

"There is a great deal that I can't remember clearly about my childhood—partly because I'm older now, partly because I suppressed a lot of painful memories as a little girl, but mostly because I have experienced a great deal of healing over the years.

"My dad was an alcoholic, though he never admitted it. Mother said he had always been a drinker. He was so sensitive to liquor he could get tipsy from just smelling it. All of his sisters were alcoholics, and his brother might have followed in the family line had it not been for his strong Baptist beliefs.

"But Mother always covered for Dad. He could be falling-down drunk, and she would say he had a bad headache or tell us that he wasn't home yet because there was a cow in the ditch. If he fell out of his chair at the dinner table, she would quietly get him to the bedroom. But she always acted as if everything was fine, and no one ever talked about it.

"We just went on with what we were doing as if nothing had happened. As a girl, I would pretend he wasn't drunk. I can't remember one holiday when Daddy wasn't sloppy drunk. He would disappear somewhere, and the rest of the family would go on and celebrate without him as if everything were OK. I guess my mother thought it was easier to ignore the problem than to make an issue of living with a husband who was in complete denial. I know that I developed strong habits of suppressing my emotions.

"Daddy was never physically abusive to our family. He adored my mother. Their family backgrounds were quite different. He had grown up on a farm. She had been well educated in music in Chicago, had sung with Lili Pons, and was ready to make her own professional singing debut when she met and fell in love with my father. If anyone had challenged her choice at that time with a question such as, 'What's wrong with your young man?' her reply would have been something like, 'What's wrong with a piano bench?'

"Daddy thought of himself as a self-made man. In many ways he was a good, moral man. He called himself a Christian. He was the head usher and an elder at church. But at home he was usually drunk, stumbling into cow manure in our barn.

"Being with him was like relating to two totally different people. Sober, he could be charming and lovable. But when he was drunk, I couldn't stand him, and I didn't *like* him at all. That bothered me. I prayed about it and the Lord told me it was OK, so long as I *loved* him.

"Although my father never abused us, he treated the animals horribly. He must have been taking out all his frustrations on them. One day, when I was about eight years old, I walked into the barn and caught my father pitchforking one of our cows! I got so angry that I grabbed the pitchfork out of his hands, stood between him and the cow, and shouted, 'You get out of here and go away, or I'll ram this thing through your body!'

"When I was older, again I stood between him and the animals, and this time I knocked him down in my ferocious anger! I didn't like knocking my father down, but when he was drunk and abusive, I couldn't see him as 'father.' There was a radical change in his personality. I felt like I was shoving someone else—a completely different person who was a threat to us all and who had to be stopped by somebody.

"I can remember so many times watching my father go into the barn and then come out like a man with no bones, disintegrating in front of my eyes. I felt confused, bewildered, and hurt.

"If I was ashamed, I didn't know it. I wasn't consciously afraid. Perhaps it was because anger overwhelmed my fear.

"Everywhere we went I was *glad* he wasn't with us!

"After I grew older, my father insisted that he had quit drinking altogether. But he continued to go on "trips," and I knew he was still in bondage to liquor. My suspicions were confirmed when I was working in the garden one day and found bottles of wine, whiskey, and cooking fuel (called "canned heat") stashed in the ground among the flowers. I could never trust him or rest in him.

### How did all of this affect my life?

"I know that I am probably as vulnerable to alcohol as anyone else in my family, but I chose not to go that way. I have always had a problem with stress. I'm gifted with a lot of creativity, and I enjoy doing many things. But I tend to become too involved. I take on too much emotional responsibility, and then I suffer from severe headaches and get rashes all over my body.

"Marriage was for me a series of disappointments and disasters. When my youngest daughter was about eight or nine, I suffered a nervous breakdown and was given shock treatments. Healing began to happen after the treatments, but my doctor told me it was my faith that made me well.

"I love the Lord, and He has worked faithfully, even miraculously at times, to heal me. Once I was expected to die, but I surprised everyone, including my physician, with a radical and 'impossible' recovery. I figured God must have more to do with me here on earth!

"My daughter has always been a healing gift to me from God. She never really seemed like a child. As she was growing up, she had a special quality of wisdom, empathy, and sympathy that she lovingly gave to me. I searched to find a good church where I could relate in a close, personal way to the Lord and His people.

"When my daughter married, she and her husband ministered deeply to me. I don't remember what happened when they prayed for me—I think I passed out—but it was powerful! After that I began to drink great gulps of healing and to experience bundles of goodness. I also had a vivid spiritual experience of sitting on God's lap. No person had ever held me like that. I am grateful for the abundance of healing I have experienced. But God isn't finished with me yet. In His wisdom He has left me with a 'barometer' and provided me with protection through my loved ones. When too many activities and concerns have been stimulating me, sparking my sensitive and overworked nervous system, tension builds, and I begin to experience a kind of frantic urgency to control my world.

"I pay attention to the symptoms and retreat to the quietness of my room. There I can spend private restorative time with my heavenly Father, who is consistently and reliably the same strong, understanding, gentle, and nurturing Abba yesterday, today, and always. And when I fail to heed the signals, my family reminds me with a loving and gentle sternness, 'Grandma, it's time to go to your room.'"

> For my father and my mother have forsaken me, but the LORD will take me up.
>
> —PSALM 27:10

## HOW TO COPE—LIVING WITH AN ALCOHOLIC

Donna's and Anna's stories are remarkable testimonies of how God can—and will—turn things around for your good. It doesn't happen overnight; sometimes there is a process to go through. But when we genuinely turn over everything to His care, then He can work on our behalf.

Perhaps you're thinking, *Paula, you have no idea what I am going through right now. I am in a living hell!* And you're right—to a degree. I don't know your personal history, but I do know there is help available.

First and foremost, ask Jesus to reveal whatever is inside of you that needs to be carried to the foot of the cross. *You are the only person you can change; you can't change anybody else.* Change has to begin in your own heart. Examine your emotions and allow yourself to feel them. It's OK to tell God that you are hurting or angry. He already knows that, but confession will set *you* free.

> For he will deliver the needy when he cries for help,
> The afflicted also, and him who has no helper.
>
> —PSALM 72:12

Then pray that He will do likewise for your loved one in order to set all of you free.

## Enablers and helpers

Most women living with alcoholics fall into one of two categories: enablers and helpers. An enabler supports an environment that allows the alcoholic to continue drinking.[1] Anna's mother, for example, was an enabler. Enablers will:

    ℰↄ    Call in sick to the alcoholic's workplace with a false reason for absence.

    ℰↄ    Make excuses to family and friends for the addict's behavior.

    ℰↄ    Cover up when the alcoholic parent misses a child's event.

The other category is a helper. A helper truly encourages the alcoholic to acknowledge his or her illness and seek treatment.[2]

If your husband, father, or loved one refuses to seek help for his alcohol addiction, then you need to show tough love. It won't be easy, but make it clear that you will no longer tolerate the way he treats you (or the family). If he continues to do so, you will need to distance yourself from him until he gets into a recovery program and seeks counseling.

If you are living with an alcoholic, here are some things you can do to cope:

    ℰↄ    Remain "up" and positive. Don't join him or her down in the dumps.

    ℰↄ    Stop taking responsibility for what your addictive spouse does.

&#8667;  Don't allow yourself or your children to be abused.

&#8667;  Find a loving, supportive church family.

&#8667;  Seek godly counsel and, if necessary, someone who will intervene.

Intervention involves meeting with friends and authorities and the addict to confront clearly, but kindly; also, have a rehabilitation program/facility reserved. Don't just *tell* the addict to go to rehab—*take* him or her, then and there.

Above all, pray and seek God's face.

## WHEN YOUR TEENAGER IS A SUBSTANCE ABUSER

As I shared earlier in chapter five, the loss of a child is a tremendous heartache. I dare say that without God's comfort and guidance, a woman going through the grieving process suffers pain too great to bear alone. Your only consolation comes from knowing that one day you will be reunited with that child in heaven.

But what if you are losing your child to drugs and/or alcohol abuse? Your pain is just as unbearable, and perhaps worse, because your child is throwing his or her life away and you feel powerless to help him or her.

In my day, substance abuse among teenagers was unheard of. Unfortunately, in today's society, drug and alcohol abuse are rampant among our youth. Daily news reports bombard us with negative details of "date rape" drugs, children sniffing bottles of glue, gumballs laced with marijuana, the increasing use of methamphetamine, and the list goes on. As I said earlier, I have never experienced any of this personally as a wife or mother, but over the years I have ministered to many women in such a situation.

I realize that there are no pat answers or guarantees that your teenager will ever come out of that lifestyle. What I do hope to accomplish is to offer you some gentle advice as a counselor and minister. Scripture tells us:

> Train up a child in the way he should go,
> Even when he is old he will not depart from it.
> —PROVERBS 22:6

But our cry is, "How old, O Lord?" We are reduced to prayer. And there is no greater power and "mountain mover" than the prayer of faith. Ask God to reveal the hidden things to you. Ask the Holy Spirit to guide you and show you if your teenager is involved in drinking or drugs, and to give you wisdom and strength to confront the situation.

> For there is nothing hidden that will not be disclosed, and nothing concealed that will not be known or brought out into the open.
> —LUKE 8:17, NIV

Next, be proactive. If you have very young children, begin praying for their future spouses and lives now. Speak blessings over them daily. Teach them from the Word, and train them to keep the Word in their hearts.

> Thy word I have treasured in my heart,
> That I may not sin against Thee.
> —PSALM 119:11

If your children are in their teens, stay involved in their lives. Know what they are doing, why, where they are going, and with whom. Get acquainted with their friends. If they say they are invited to a party, ask to speak with the adult/parent who is hosting it before allowing them to go. Don't forget to praise and reward your child for good behavior.

Make your expectations clear about how you feel. For example, "I don't want you doing alcohol, smoking, or taking drugs of any kind." Set the ground rules, and make sure your child understands that there are consequences for breaking them. If he or she breaks the rule, carry through with your discipline.

Be a role model to your children. Remember, if you don't model abstinence and righteousness, then your admonitions will have little effect on your children.

Here are some telltale signs to know if your teenager is using drugs:

- Negative changes in schoolwork

- Increased secrecy about possessions or activities

- Use of room deodorants or perfumes to hide the smoke and chemical odors

- Bottle of eyedrops used to mask bloodshot eyes or dilated pupils

- Evidence of drug paraphernalia[3]

As a parent, you are the single most important influence in your teenager's life. Take action *now* before it's too late.

When talking to your child about alcohol or drugs, let him or her know that you love him/her and are worried that he/she might be using drugs or alcohol. Let them know you are there to listen to them and that you want to help them.

Be sure that you are calm and collected in your thoughts before approaching him/her. If you rant and yell, your child will tune you out or rant and yell back. That is obviously counter-productive. You want them to hear what you have to say. But be compassionate with your teenager, so that he or she knows for certain that you are for, and not against, him or her.

End your discussion by praying with him/her; speak words of blessing over his/her life. Later, apart from the teenager, pray for the spirit of strife and discord to be gone from your home, and ask God to bring unity into your family.

You may feel lonely, but you are never alone.

*Chapter 8*

# SINGLE, *but* NOT ALONE

B RENDA WORKED FOR OUR ministry at Elijah House for several years. She was a beautiful, intelligent, insightful young woman in her thirties who profoundly blessed many with her gifts of counseling and prayer. Almost everyone was puzzled by the fact that she remained single.

She had a lovely face and figure, and her shiny auburn hair would have qualified her to pose for shampoo commercials. She dressed tastefully and attractively. Her bright personality was charming. She was conversant on a variety of subjects. Several counselees commented that they couldn't understand why men weren't lined up at her door.

I'm not describing a superwoman who possessed an unflawed personality with whom no one could identify. Like the rest of us, she had wounds in her heart that needed to be healed and habits that had to be transformed. At that time there was a privateness about her that did not allow many to know her intimately. But neither was there a sign on her forehead telling people to remain at a distance.

Because Brenda was an excellent teacher and as a single could identify with the feelings of singles, we asked her to address the singles' issues at a seminar. I will never forget the response she received when she stated emphatically, "There *is* life after puberty!" The audience erupted in waves of laughter. And the people settled in to hear Brenda's message, which said again and again in many ways that our basic security, wholeness, value, and effectiveness as persons—whether we are married or single—depend upon our developing relationship with the Lord Jesus Christ.

He is the one who gives us power to confront and overcome the hurtful and often crippling circumstances of life; He is able to transform our weaknesses into strengths. Though you may be single, having many attendant struggles and frustrations, you are not rejected, and you are *never* alone.

Brenda eventually married, became a mother, and continued her ministry. She is not a whole person because she found a marriage partner. She became a good marriage partner because she was whole in Christ before she married.

## HEART CRIES FROM HURTING SINGLES

Perhaps you can relate to Brenda's story with the exception of her "happily ever after." You are still waiting for the right one to come along.

Throughout our years of counseling, John and I have heard from hurting singles. Here are the most common expressions we've heard.

*"I'm past forty, my biological clock is ticking, and time is running out. My chances of becoming a mother are fading fast."*

Most women who share this cry simply endure the disappointment and then develop ways of coping. Some become loving "aunts" or "best grown-up friends" to their friends' children. Our children were not able to be with their own natural grandparents very often because they lived hundreds of miles away. But they were always blessed by surrogate grandmothers in the church who took delight in loving them.

Some single women become gifted teachers or youth workers. God can find many ways to enable a barren woman to become the joyful mother of children (Ps. 113:9). If you have already "adopted" and nurtured many children and still find an empty ache rising from deep inside—an unsatisfied longing for your *own*, know that your feelings are normal. God understands and wants to comfort your heart.

The natural desire in a woman to bring forth life is so powerful that today increasing numbers of single women are deliberately becoming pregnant because of their overwhelming desire to mother a child. Often they have become so wounded, rejected, and hardened that they care very little about whose seed they receive. They never intended to live in a sustained covenant relationship with the father.

For them, the pain of barrenness is so intense that they choose to bring a baby into the world for the sake of their own comfort and fulfillment with no consideration for the deep wounding this can inflict on the spirit of their baby. Every child needs both a father and a mother. Children so conceived begin life with a seed of rejection and a sense of being used.

Until these wounds are healed, they will be crippled in their ability to receive the love the mother felt she was so desperate to give. And until her self-centered motives are discovered, repented of, and forgiven, the quality of love the mother tries to express will be seriously warped by its self-serving nature.

### *"I grieve for the babies I've never had—as if they had been born and died!"*

I nearly wept as I heard this cry. Here was a lovely woman, just past forty. She was attractive, a rare mixture of gentleness and strength. Her life had been invested for years in a ministry that brought people to life, and she had learned well the meaning of love in spending herself for the sake of others.

There was no question that she had become the mother of many spiritual children. But she was grieving for her *own*. My heart broke for her as I identified with her sense of loss. She had truly conceived in her imagination and labored to bring forth her children in the deep longing of her dreams, but they were stillborn (figuratively speaking), and she had never held them in her arms. She was fearful she never would.

She was trying not to be angry, but the thought kept coming to her: *What a waste that I have all this reproductive equipment inside of me! What a useless bother to live through biological cycles that produce nothing but discomfort!* I kept thinking what a fine mother she could be and wondering what had happened to the husband God may have intended for her.

My heart cried out, "O God, if he is out there, let them find one another quickly." I don't know if you too grieve for the children you have never borne. I do know, however, that God is ready to comfort you and wrap His loving arms around you. He promises you in His Word:

> "Shout for joy, O barren one, you who have borne no
> child;

> Break forth into joyful shouting and cry aloud, you who
>     have not travailed;
> For the sons of the desolate one will be more numerous
> Than the sons of the married woman," says the LORD.
>                                           —ISAIAH 54:1

For now, focus on the children God does bring into your life during this time. Pour out your love on them; you will not be disappointed.

***"I love the Lord. I love my work. I have lots of friends. But I always wanted to have my own family. There's an empty place in me that nothing really satisfies."***

This is the complaint we have heard most often from women serving as singles on the mission field. They are usually attractive, talented, and dedicated women who would not be satisfied with ordinary jobs just to bring in a paycheck. They sincerely want to invest their lives in serving the Lord and setting others free. Most of them feel called by God in some way to do that.

But rarely have we met anyone who would not admit that she had always dreamed of doing the same sort of work alongside a husband—and *children*—sharing work, play, joys, and sorrows together.

Some on the field were perhaps not first "called" in the sense of God giving them a clear directive to go. It was rather the loss of a husband through death or divorce that propelled them into searching for meaningful places to invest their lives. God then met them where they were and opened a door. But they still feel a personal need for love with skin on it.

There are women who choose from the beginning to invest their lives in careers rather than in nurturing a family. They become so busy and pour themselves so completely into becoming successful businesswomen, decorators, teachers, scientists, journalists, and the like that for years they pay no attention to what lies hidden beneath their conscious focus. Then as retirement years approach, they begin to recognize that there is a part of them that has never had a chance to live. Some seem to be content to remain as they are. Others find their successes and laurels painfully lacking in human warmth.

One brilliant and talented single woman pointed to her PhD certificate framed on the wall of her study and said to me with tears in her eyes, "As I grow older, I'm having a terrible time trying to cuddle up to that."

*"I get so hungry for someone to hold me, someone to talk to, someone to go places with, to share important things, to pray with, to grow old with."*

The woman who made this comment had been married and had raised several children. But her marriage had ended in divorce, and her children had grown up and moved away. She was fearful that the intensity of her unmet needs might propel her into an inappropriate or premature relationship.

At least she was aware of her vulnerability and was seeking help. Many women are not. They are simply driven by feelings that block out discernment. Many more avoid seeking counsel because they fear misunderstanding and condemnation. Condemnation is entirely inappropriate. These feelings are natural.

Not only did God design you, as a woman, with a *need for* love, but He also created you to fulfill man, to nurture and protect his heart. "The heart of her husband trusts in her, and he will have no lack of gain" (Prov. 31:11). When you are denied that opportunity, you are also denied the expression of a part of who you are. Whether or not you can identify it clearly, your sense of intrinsic worth is damaged.

Whether you have never married, were married but lost your husband, or are married but your husband's inability to be intimate shuts you out of his heart, you share the same basic hurt and frustration as all other women walking the path alone.

You are blocked from becoming all you were created to be. Man and woman were both created for togetherness. But it seems to me that, generally speaking, we tend to naturally gravitate more easily to intimacy while men tend to flee.

### *"Obviously I'm not good-looking—no one has chosen me."*

This comment tumbled from the mouth of an unusually attractive woman who was just about to celebrate her fortieth birthday. She very capably occupied a position of responsibility in an outstandingly reputable international service organization. People not only treated her with respect and honor, but they also called her "friend."

But she felt ugly because no man had chosen her as a wife. Though she had dated from time to time, no serious relationship had ever developed. My husband and I tried to affirm her beauty as we could so clearly see it.

She appreciated our effort, but all the persuasive affirmation in the world could not have changed the "facts" she had identified as truth. Therefore, in her mind, she "knew" no one would choose her because of her appearance. Sadly, she opted to believe the lie that the enemy had fed her.

Ironically, the opposite is often true. It is the very fact that you *are* beautiful and you *are* achieving a level of success that intimidates men. They feel inadequate, small, and as if they have nothing to offer you. They fear you might reject them, and nothing is more detrimental to a man's ego than rejection. You may ask, "Paula, does that mean I have to lower my standards, look 'uglier,' or act as if I don't know anything?" Absolutely not!

You are the woman God designed you to be even before you were born—with all of your physical, mental, and spiritual attributes. And perhaps someday that special someone will come into your life when God deems the time to be right. But it will be someone who values you and appreciates you *for who you are.*

## POSSIBLE ANSWERS FOR OFTEN-ASKED *WHYS*

"If there is someone out there for me, then why haven't I found him?" How often have I heard that! But whether you have never married or you are single again through divorce (which I will cover in the next chapter) or death, your pain is very real, and God can restore your soul if you allow Him.

Our son Mark was a student at Denver Theological Seminary. Mark was impatient and somewhat angry because he was almost twenty-nine without having found the love of his life. His three brothers had been happily married at nineteen, twenty, and twenty-one. He was glad for their sakes but wondered why he wasn't being so blessed.

Mark had a number of friends who happened to be girls, but no romantic interest developed in the relationships. Family and friends would try to encourage him with, "She's out there somewhere, Mark. I just know it." And he would reply, "I've heard that before, and I'd like to believe it!" I was concerned for the growing anger and despair in his attitude, and one day as I was praying for him, the Lord clearly led me to read Psalm 128:2–3.

When you shall eat of the fruit of your hands, you will be happy and it will be well with you. Your wife shall be like a fruitful vine within your house, your children like olive plants around your table.

I copied the scripture and gave it to Mark, saying I believed that the Lord meant it for him. He carried it in his Bible.

Meanwhile Maureen, who eventually became Mark's wife, was watching her twenties passing by quickly, and though she was encouraged to be receiving some healing for early wounds in her life, she also was impatient and frustrated, wondering if she would ever find the right man.

John went to Calgary, Alberta, to teach, and Maureen was in the audience. She asked God to send her a husband like John. (She didn't know that Mark is in many ways more like John than even John realizes.)

Later one of our staff members counseled with Maureen, and in the process of their conversation, the counselor happened to mention Mark's name. Maureen knew in her spirit that someday she would marry him.

Not long after that, Maureen attended a course at a church where they were studying our books. They asked her name and then inquired as to why she had come. She answered, "I'm here because God is preparing me to marry Mark Sandford." The people were a bit startled, but they didn't challenge her. I don't know whether it was because she sounded so confident or because they thought she was a bit strange.

Maureen eventually came to Coeur d'Alene, Idaho, for counseling. Mark was home at the time, doing an internship with Elijah House. We sent him to meet Maureen as she disembarked the plane. Two lonely people were zapped that night, and they talked until nearly two in the morning. That began a courtship that continued mostly by letter and telephone over the next nine months.

Eventually, Mark and Maureen married. Maureen never returned to Canada. Since their marriage, we have seen both of them blossoming, bringing out the best in one another, with a beautiful family besides.

What is the moral of this story? *God's timing!* Mark was a late bloomer. He had been molested as a little child. In him were deep memories he had totally suppressed. In the first few weeks of their marriage, the Holy Spirit brought those memories to his consciousness.

Maureen also had deep wounds that needed the healing oil of the Lord's Spirit. The Lord's love between them had prepared their hearts to minister to one another. At just the right time in the maturation and healing process, God brought them together. If they had found each other earlier, neither would have been prepared to meet the other sensitively, and issues rising from past wounds would have seriously hindered intimacy. It could have been a disaster instead of a celebration.

I believe that often when the Lord doesn't seem to answer the anxious and impatient prayers of His children, it is His kindness and His mercy that hold His answers back. If you are able to take a risk, and you are willing to do what you're doing and wait, trusting in Him, then He will answer you in His time.

## ROADBLOCKS TO WHOLENESS

You may ask, "What if there's something in me that is preventing me from meeting the right person?" It could very well be that there are blockages in you. Some of the most common are:

1. The emotional wounds you have received

2. The lies you have accepted

3. The judgments you have made

4. The expectations you have developed

5. The walls you have built

6. The inner vows you have made

7. The unconscious messages you send

The good news is that you don't have to continue to live with any of them. You can be set free. First, let's examine what might be causing these blockages; then we will learn how to deal with them.

### What wounds?

From the time of your conception you have within you a sensitive personal spirit that knows whether you were invited or an accident. If you experienced a lot of love in your home as a child, you rest in that love, but if your parents were constantly quarreling, then you tensed up in fear and hurt.

Children are extremely sensitive emotionally and spiritually to the atmosphere of a home. Perhaps as a child you knew early on whether you were viewed as a blessing or an intrusive burden by the way your parents responded to your needs with gratitude—or griping. You felt chosen as they delighted in being with you, or you carry deep wounds because of their neglect or physical and verbal abuse during your early years.

If your parents were affectionate, then you are filled with

love and strength of spirit to face life. If there was unconditional love balanced with appropriate discipline, the question
of belonging is settled at deep levels in your spirit. You developed the courage and security to venture, to make mistakes,
and to try again.

Without these basic gifts of acceptance and nurture, your
spirit withers like a plant that receives too little water and
sunshine. If you were continually lacerated by criticism, you
may curl up and die emotionally, becoming a puddle of rejection, an apology for being. Or you may lash out in hurt and
anger and strive either to show them or shame them.

If your parents (especially your father) told you, as you were
growing up, that you were beautiful and how proud they were
of you, you *know* that you are beautiful. But if no one told you
how lovely you are and instead ridiculed you, you may see
yourself as ugly and ashamed even though you are built to win
beauty contests.

### What lies?

Perhaps you have accepted the lie that you have no right
to exist. You have been fed the lie that you will have to earn
love to get any in return. You have believed the lie that you
are worthy of love only if you do everything right (whatever "right" means). You were a mistake, an intrusion, and
a burden, so you don't belong. You chose to believe there is
something dreadfully wrong with you, that you are ugly and
rejected. You believe you are somehow responsible for the
sins of your parents, and, therefore, you don't really deserve
blessing.

### What judgments?

It is one thing to recognize and rightly judge something or someone to be immoral, unjust, and hurtful. It is another matter to judge in a condemning way as you wallow in hate and anger.

While we are not responsible for the sins of others, we will be held accountable for our own responses and for the attitudes to which we cling.

### What expectations?

Maybe you have always felt as if no one ever loved you or treated you with sensitivity. You've always had to look out for yourself, because if you didn't, then who would?

No matter how hard you work or how good a job you do, you expect to be criticized. You feel as if you are not smart enough or sharp enough, so you expect to be passed over. You strive to win people's acceptance, to feel as if you belong, only to be rejected anyway (or at least, that is how you perceive it).

Those wounds you carry have lowered your expectations of what you want out of life, of your perception of others, and, most importantly, your perception of self.

### What walls?

Walls not only keep out those things we don't want, but they also keep all of our feelings in.

When you have been wounded, you learn to build defensive walls to protect your feelings. You harden your heart and refuse, often unconsciously, to let anyone in beyond a certain point. Maybe you gladly serve others and minister to their wants, but that simply allows you to preserve some measure of control.

We maintain ourselves as very private people, hiding our own needs, hurts, and fears because, if we open our hearts, we become vulnerable to the imperfections of others. We choose the pain of loneliness and isolation rather than risk the possibility of violation or betrayal.

Unfortunately, a wall is a wall. Walls not only keep out the bad, but they block out the good as well. Ezekiel 36:26 and 11:19 both say that Jesus will take out of us the "heart of stone" and give us a "heart of flesh." He offers us the protection of His breastplate of righteousness (Eph. 6:14). But we are so afraid of giving up the security of our own defenses that when good times and loving people have begun to melt our hearts, we may suddenly stop in the midst of celebrating new freedoms and fellowships to flee back to our familiar prison.

### What vows?

Sometimes a person or situation leaves such a deep wound that we make a vow never to allow another person or situation like that to enter our lives again. We may say things like:

- "I opened my heart to trust once and was betrayed. I will *never* trust again."

- "It hurts to be rejected. I will reject before I am rejected."

- "I shared my feelings, and people used them against me. I will hide my feelings."

- "My mother was a doormat for my father. I will never let anyone walk on me like that."

Such strong vows made early in life are indicators of an area we choose to block off from our inner being. They become programmed into our psyche, to be recalled later in life when our "buttons" are pushed in similar circumstances. The vows then drive us to respond compulsively.

### What subconscious messages?

At other times you may be sending subconscious messages such as, "You don't like me. You won't choose me; no one ever has. You'll reject me. You'll go away; everyone does. I can't trust you. I'll not need you. Go ahead and hit me; I won't cry. I can take care of myself."

What does your body language say? Do you walk with your head down looking at the ground, or do you walk with your head up? God has made you the head and not the tail (Deut. 28:13). Say to yourself, "But Thou, O LORD, art a shield about me, my glory, and the *One who lifts my head*" (Ps. 3:3, emphasis added). The way you carry yourself and your tone of voice both send a message to people of how you view yourself.

## "SO WHAT CAN I DO?"

What can you do to get rid of these roadblocks (as they apply to you)?

First and foremost, pray. James 5:16 says, "Confess your sins to one another, and pray for one another, so that you may be healed." It is essentially that simple. With others, and then in personal discipline, pray:

> 1. That the Lord will pour His love into the depths of the spirit of the wounded child you have been

and cause love to abide there as a holy, healing medicine.

2. That the lies you accepted about yourself be brought to death on the cross and that you be set free to see and embrace yourself as Jesus does.

3. In repentance for any condemning judgments you made, especially against your parents. Make choices to forgive, and expect Jesus to make those choices a reality.

4. That you renounce your practiced expectations. Ask for a new and right spirit within.

5. That the Lord will melt the walls of your heart and cause your fleshly defenses to crumble so that you may be protected by His breastplate and shield as you step forward into vulnerability and unfamiliar territory.

6. Taking authority over the inner vows you have made, breaking their influence over you.

7. That the old messages that misrepresented the desires of your heart and blocked God's plan for you be obliterated—and that new messages of blessing and invitation issue from you under the direction of the Holy Spirit.

Then begin walking in your prayers! Prayer is the key to removing the roadblocks on your way to wholeness.

## SUPPORT GROUPS

Another way to help you overcome these obstacles is to foster healthy, vital relationships through well-balanced support groups.

### Family-type groups

Some of the richest experiences in a Christian group happen in groups that are diversified—young and old, male and female, married and single. These small group structures can provide friendship and nurture for singles.

In such a group, you can enjoy the sense of family-type nurturing you may not have received in your own natural family. If your family wounded you, now you have the chance to be healed through prayer and to enjoy a new experience with people who have been equipped to model healthy relationships for you, to carry you in their hearts, and to love you for life. Your new family can, with unconditional love, build into you a Christian identity and self-esteem in order for you to become all that you can be.

If you have children, there are likely to be male role models—grandfather- or big-brother-types—within the group from whom your children can learn and emulate how a godly man should act.

### Singles' groups

Ideally, singles' groups should offer opportunities for people to gather to meet people and experience refreshing and supportive fellowship that takes the edge off loneliness. They should provide a measure of security in belonging—and offer healing ministry to those who seek it.

If singles' groups create a wholesome environment of fun and adventure, meaningful conversation, recreation, and stimulating corporate study and service projects, lasting relationships will have an opportunity to develop.

All groups, single or otherwise, need some sort of focus outside themselves, or else they can easily become self-seeking or problem-centered—depending on the security, self-esteem, and stability of those who are a part of them.

John and I have seen some very healthy singles' groups. We have had the privilege of participating in a number of beautiful weddings, and we have watched the positive growth of marriages birthed in such groups. But we have also listened to many tales of disappointment and disillusionment. Probably the comment most often heard and made is, "I went to a Christian singles' group to *meet* other people and make friends, but instead it turned out to be a *meat* market!"

While the term "meat market" may offend some readers, reality is that this is all too often the case. I do not mean to paint a critical picture of singles' groups. On the contrary, as I stated earlier, we have seen much good fruit produced in them. We have prayed with many young men and women who are earnestly searching for wholesome and lasting relationships to find one another somewhere in the midst of our modern culture.

We simply have to recognize that we live in a world where the absoluteness of God's law has been eroded from the culture and where illicit sex has been incessantly portrayed in the media as the desirable norm.

Too often Christians have imposed sexual taboos on our teenagers and young adults, with no real communication concerning the blessed holiness of marital sex. The power of a dictatorial "no-no" in the life of a teenager who is in the process of individuating from her or his parents is the force to drive her or him into rebellion, and thus into extreme vulnerability to peer pressure.

If the world continues to boldly and skillfully deliver the delusive message that sex is OK in *whatever* circumstance or relationship, and if no one tells our young people about the sexual glory the Lord designed for them within the parameters of a godly marriage, then how can our young people know the truth? How can they understand that they are exchanging their birthright for a miserable and sickening mess of pottage?

Secular sex education has attempted to arm students with information for the protection of their physical well-being. But God is calling Christians to understand and speak clearly concerning the relationship between the sexuality and spirituality of every person, especially as we are equipped or unequipped to enter into real intimacy.

## SEX AND THE SINGLE

If God Himself invented sex and it was His idea, then why are we having such problems? People don't understand the relationship of body and spirit. It is impossible for one person to touch another only physically. Our personal spirit is not poured into our body like water into a container. Our personal spirit gives life to our body (James 2:26) and flows through all its cells. Therefore, when we touch another, our spirit is also involved.

> Or do you not know that the one who joins himself to a harlot *is one body with her?* For He says, *"The two will become one flesh."* But the one who joins himself to the Lord is one spirit with Him. Flee immorality. Every other sin that a man commits is outside the body, but the

immoral man sins against his own body. Or do you not know that your body is a temple of the Holy Spirit who is in you, whom you have from God, and that you are not your own? For you have been bought with a price: therefore glorify God in your body.

—1 CORINTHIANS 6:16–20, *emphasis added*

God has created husbands and wives to become one flesh in holy covenantal union (Gen. 2:24; Eph. 5:31). He has so built a man that, in union with his wife, his spirit reaches out to enfold, protect, and nurture her. A woman is built to embrace and nurture her husband.

When two people become "one flesh" in an unholy union, their spirits latch on to one another because that is what their spirits were created to do. Adulterers and fornicators meet in sinful perversion of God's intent. They have not been given His permission and blessing in marriage, and thus they cannot complete one another in holiness. Their union tells lies one to the other about who they are, and it causes them to carry confusion within them from their coming together.

If a person has lain with many partners, it becomes impossible to bond with that person because his or her spirit's focus and energies are scattered, seeking the many with whom he or she was joined. Therefore, wherever there has been an unholy union, or worse, a molestation, pray that the Lord Himself will wield His sword of truth to separate the two spirits so that each can be free to be wholly given to his or her own mate.

Following the guidance of the Holy Spirit, pray, in the name of Jesus, that the person's spirit will forget the union. The mind may never forget, but the spirit needs to be set free from the emotional ties. Many for whom we have prayed in this way have exclaimed, "I feel so *together*. I didn't realize how scattered I was!"

Many singles think that being sexually active before

marriage will equip them to be better lovers after marriage. As a counselor I can tell you that it is just the opposite. When they marry, they have countless problems.

They have forfeited the discovery of the wonder of physical intimacy in the light of God's blessing, the unspoiled treasure of privateness, the sharing with one another what is theirs and theirs alone.

They are severely crippled in their ability to bond. Until they have repented and the Lord sets them free, they drag to the marriage bed shadows of every sexual encounter they ever had. However good that sexual encounter may have seemed, it *cannot* have carried with it the glory God intends for a man and his wife to share.

As a couple come together in a holy union, meeting and embracing one another in complete intimacy, the Holy Spirit moves to sing through each person's spirit and then as an exhilarative gift and a holy blessing of love. *The Holy Spirit will not sing in immoral places!*

> Drink water from your own cistern, and fresh water from your own well. Should your springs be dispersed abroad, streams of water in the streets? Let them be yours alone, and not for strangers with you. Let your fountain be blessed, and *rejoice in the wife of your youth. As a loving hind and a graceful doe, let her breasts satisfy you at all times; be exhilarated always with her love.* For why should you, my son, be exhilarated with an adulteress, and embrace the bosom of a foreigner? For the ways of a man are before the eyes of the LORD, and He watches all his paths. His own iniquities will capture the wicked, and he will be held with the cords of his sin. He will die for lack of instruction, and in the greatness of his folly he will go astray.
> —PROVERBS 5:15–23, *emphasis added*

God wants us to enjoy sex within the confines of marriage. His moral laws are guidelines for our protection so that we don't corrupt, distort, and lose His good gifts.

## GUIDELINES FOR REMAINING PURE

It's not easy being single. Unfortunately for many, when their hormones turn on, their brains fall out, and they follow passion into a mess of confusion and hurt. As I have already explained, there is a way back to sanity and holiness through the forgiveness and the healing power of Jesus. Here are some practical suggestions to help you remain pure.

### Set boundaries for yourself.

How far will you go with a man who is not your husband? When passions begin to rise—*stop!* Notice I used the word *begin.* In other words, don't wait until you are in the heat of the moment to stop something that should never have started in the first place. The road of passion leads to covenant relationship. Covenant is forever.

### Don't fall for anyone's line.

Don't believe the line, "If you love me, you will..." If he *really* loves you, he will *wait,* respecting you. You might say, "I feel as if we're already married in spirit." Great, but wait until the rest of you gets married, and don't set too long an engagement period.

### *Wait for God's choice for you.*

Waiting is probably one of the hardest choices you face as a single. God may very well have the right person out there for you. Pray that God will bring him into your life in God's time, and ask for discernment to recognize him when he arrives. Keep yourself clean for his sake. Don't let any shopper handle the merchandise until he has signed the papers.

### *If you're engaged, wait until after marriage.*

Even when you are sure you have found the right one and are engaged, be determined not to dull the excitement and intrigue of your honeymoon. So many young ladies think it's OK, because they're getting married within a few months. If they are already engaged in a sexual relationship before marriage, then where are the surprises on the honeymoon?

### *Stay out of parked cars and other dark, isolated places.*

In case you haven't noticed, we girls can do quite a bit of long-term hugging without going overboard; guys are not made that way. Instead of sitting in a parked car or being alone with him, try bicycling or playing a sport, like tennis, together. Go out on group or double dates. Learn to become friends before becoming lovers. John and I have been happily (and still romantically) married for more than fifty years. We were friends before we were lovers.

### *Look for positive opportunities to share your God-given abilities.*

If nothing seems to be happening for you, don't fantasize or dwell on your frustrations or unfulfilled dreams. Focus outward. Meet people. Make friends by being one, and invest yourself in some sort of support group. Take hold of every healthy opportunity for life that comes your way (remembering that this is not anything like "any port in a storm"; God wants you to have His best).

### *Pray for a temporary gift of celibacy.*

It's a viable solution and a good gift. Without a gift of celibacy, many go on to follow desire and temptation into illicit sex, which may result in HIV or some other sexually transmitted disease. Some who strive to be celibate without the gift either lose their ability to function or fear that they will.

ের

God did not design us to be alone. He created us with the need for fellowship and intimacy. Being single can be a blessing, but so can a godly marriage. When we heed His Word, we can experience a holy union. When one partner (or most often, both) fails to obey Him, then she or he invites the heartache of divorce. But even in divorce, God's mercy is still available if you seek Him.

# Chapter 9

## GOD'S MERCY
### *for the* DIVORCÉE

WHEN YOU WALKED DOWN the aisle on your
wedding day, I am sure that, as you looked at your
beloved and said, "I do," the last thing on your
mind was the thought that you might be divorced some day.
No woman dreams of going through the pain, the anguish, and
the betrayal that follow divorce. When you divorced, it was as
if a part of you died.

Unfortunately, divorce has become far more prevalent
within the church than it has in the world. The number of
divorces among believers is almost on a par with nonbelievers.
What is so tragic is that, far too often, singles in the church
who were married and are now divorced feel like outcasts.
They are made to feel as if they have committed the unforgivable sin. And the church has put limitations on them, especially in the area of ministry.

Let me begin by saying divorce is *not* the unforgivable sin. If
it were, then a possible way out of a miserable marriage might

be to murder your spouse! A wife could be forgiven the sin of murder and go on with her life in the more acceptable state of widowhood. In that role she would be legally free to marry, and someday someone might even ask her to give her testimony at a Christian ladies' luncheon.

Forgive me if this offends you. I am in no way making light of the seriousness of marriage vows or of the absoluteness of God's law. God hates divorce (Mal. 2:16), but He *does not* hate the divorcée! He hates the pain and anguish that not only the divorcée but also all the family and close friends have to walk through. He knows what devastating pain it is because He Himself has borne our grief and carried our sorrows (Isa. 53:4).

The other half of Malachi 2:16 goes on to say, "…and him who covers his garment with wrong." Granted, there are many who have made no real effort to reconcile their troubled marriage, and then go from one relationship to another without ever coming to awareness or repentance for sinful and dysfunctional areas of their own hearts.

Our modern-day culture has made it easy to do that by desensitizing people to the grief their self-centered actions bring to others, especially their children, and to God. "They cover their garments with wrong" can be verbalized according to the strongholds of the day: "I deserve some happiness." "He/she doesn't understand me." "My children would be better off without me." "I need to be free so I can find out who I am."

But I plead the question, "Is such self-centered flippancy the sin of *all* who have gone through divorce?" Absolutely not! And even if it were, would that excuse Christians who cover their own garments with wrong in the form of condemning judgment projected upon divorced people?

Jesus Himself called us to "be merciful, just as your Father is merciful." Immediately He went on to add, "And do not judge and you will not be judged; and do not condemn, and you will not be condemned; pardon, and you will be pardoned" (Luke 6:36–37). And yet divorced people are made to feel like outcasts or second-class citizens in many congregations, rather than receiving much-needed ministry from those whom God has designed and called to be His healing body.

## WHY, GOD, WHY?

I don't have to explain to you how the death of a marriage usually carries with it much the same grief you would experience over the loss of a loved one by physical death. But divorce can be even more devastating because of feelings of failure, rejection, and betrayal.

Even though there is sometimes a tremendous sense of relief to be out of a situation where rancor and abuse have repeatedly caused hearts to bleed uncontrollably, a multi-residue of emotional sicknesses is likely to remain. See if you can identify with any of these comments:

> ᭲ "I made a bad choice. Can I trust my judgment again? Why didn't I recognize the danger signals while I might still have done something about them?"

> ᭲ "I couldn't live with him. But how will I live without him? I can't face being alone for the rest of my life."

> ᭲ "I'm vulnerable and am afraid of my own neediness. I'm smart enough to know that 'any port in a storm' would spell trouble for

me, but I don't really know what I'd do if some smooth operator showed up with warm persuasion and caught me in a weak moment."

CR  "What do I do with my sexual drive? Sometimes I feel lustful—not toward anyone in particular. My feelings are just there. I feel guilty for having them, but I don't know what to do with them, and I feel dirty. Sometimes I'm afraid people can see inside of me, and I want to hide."

CR  "Maybe I *should* hide. My husband didn't like me. Maybe there *is* something wrong with me. I surely don't feel attractive."

CR  "Sometimes I wish I could just die and go to heaven. I don't feel like I belong here. Even some of our old *close* friends get uptight when I'm around—as if I was a potential husband-snatcher. Or they avoid me, as if hanging around would force them to take sides."

Even more painful are the ramifications on children of divorce:

CR  "What have I done to my children? Can I ever make it up to them? What if they hate me for not making a safe nest for them? I hope they don't think it's their fault."

CR  "How can I take care of my kids? Child support won't be enough to supplement what

I can make. Will we have to move? What if my
car breaks down? What if something happens
to me? What will the kids do?"

    ఴ   "My children need a father. Is it all right for me
to remarry? What does the Bible say? What
does the church say? What would people think
of me?"

    The questions go on *ad infinitum*—to the point of exhaustion. Who can sleep restfully? What *does* the Bible say about
divorce?

## THE BIBLE'S POSITION ON DIVORCE

I believe we need to address this question from within the
context of the Eastern culture in which the Bible was written;
otherwise, we resort to legalism and miss the essential elements
of God's purpose for the Law. The Law was given primarily to
protect you, not to punish you!

> For centuries it has been possible for a husband in Arab
> lands to divorce his wife by a spoken word. The wife
> thus divorced is entitled to all her wearing apparel, and
> the husband cannot take from her anything that she
> has upon her own person. For this reason, coins on the
> headgear, and rings and necklaces, became important
> in the hour of the divorced woman's great need. This is
> one reason why there is so much interest in the bride's
> personal adornment in Eastern countries. Such customs
> of divorce were no doubt prevalent in Gentile lands in
> Old Testament times. It was for this reason that the law
> of Moses limited the power of the husband to divorce

his wife, by requiring that he must give her a *written* bill of divorcement (Deut. 24:1). Thus the Jewish custom of divorce was superior to the Arabic.

It is important to remember that the sin of adultery did not have anything to do with the matter of divorce under Jewish law. That sin was punishable by death (Lev. 20:10; Deut. 22:22), and that by stoning. If a husband found any unseemly thing in his wife, he could give her a written bill of divorcement, which made it possible for her to marry another man (Deut. 24:2). A man guilty of unfaithfulness was considered to be a criminal only in that he had invaded the rights of another man. A woman was not allowed to divorce her husband. The prophet Malachi taught that God hated "putting away," and condemned severely any man who dealt treacherously with the wife of his covenant (Mal. 2:14–16). Such was the attitude of the Hebrew people on the subject of divorce. The Lord Jesus swept away all grounds for divorce under the Law, and made unfaithfulness the lone grounds for divorce under the Christian dispensation (Matt. 5:31–32).[1]

Notice the progression in favor of protecting women from the abusive whims of men who would treat them simply as chattel and put them away for anything that, in the eyes of a displeased husband, could be said to appear to be "unseemly."

Jesus said in Matthew 19:9, "And I say to you, whoever divorces his wife, *except for immorality* [Greek, *moixeuo*, which means "adultery"], and marries another woman commits adultery" (emphasis added). The same message was given in Matthew 5:31–32, with the added comment that if the man divorces his wife for any reason other than unchastity, he *makes* her commit adultery, and whoever marries a divorced woman commits adultery.

Even the disciples, steeped in traditional ways of thinking, objected to the new restriction on men. "The disciples said to Him, 'If the relationship of the man with his wife is like this, it is better not to marry'" (Matt. 19:10).

What more powerful deterrent could be given to prevent a woman from becoming the victim of a husband who could not (largely because of cultural tradition) fully see her as a person but more like a thing to serve his pleasure! If she were put away, she and her family would carry the shame of it. And though she would be obliged to remarry, she could not then marry well, nor could she marry with honor.

As I wrote earlier, Jesus began to restore the relationship between men and women to God's original design. Paul continued in that track. Today, in many countries of the world, a woman is allowed to initiate divorce on the same grounds as her husband.

As men and women truly learn to walk in the Lord's Holy Spirit, there should be more and more ability to respect and cherish the unique person of the other. By the same token, there should be a great deal more reverence in the hearts of God's people for the eternal laws of God. But reverence for God's law is worlds away from legalism.

### *The letter of the law kills.*

We must understand that the same God who gave us the Law is also He who:

> ...made us adequate as servants of a new covenant, not of the letter, but of the Spirit, for the letter kills, but the Spirit gives life.
>
> —2 CORINTHIANS 3:6

### Our Lord is by nature a God of mercy.

> But God, being rich in mercy, because of His great love with which He loved us, even when we were dead in our transgressions, made us alive together with Christ (by grace you have been saved)...
>
> —EPHESIANS 2:4–5

### God does not owe us an explanation for His acts of mercy.

> I will have mercy on whom I have mercy, and I will have compassion on whom I have compassion.
>
> —ROMANS 9:15

### God's people are called to express His mercy.

> Be merciful, just as your Father is merciful.
>
> —LUKE 6:36

> For judgment will be merciless to one who has shown no mercy; mercy triumphs over judgment.
>
> —JAMES 2:13

## "BUT MY HUSBAND IS NOT A BELIEVER!"

Sometimes one partner believes she (or he) is justified in leaving the other simply because he (or she) is not a believer. Often they misquote 2 Corinthians 6:14, which says, "Do not be unequally yoked together with unbelievers" (NKJV), as an excuse for justifying the divorce. As I said above, as God's people, we are called to express mercy, and that includes our unsaved spouse. If we can partake of the merciful heart of our Lord, then we will have no trouble accepting what Paul says:

For the unbelieving husband is sanctified through his wife, and the unbelieving wife is sanctified through her believing husband; for otherwise your children are unclean, but now they are holy. *Yet if the unbelieving one leaves, let him leave; the brother or the sister is not under bondage in such cases, but God has called us to peace.* For how do you know, O wife, whether you will save your husband? Or how do you know, O husband, whether you will save your wife? Only, *as the Lord has assigned to each one, as God has called each, in this manner let him walk.* And thus I direct in all the churches.
—1 CORINTHIANS 7:14–17, *emphasis added*

Belief certainly involves more than what we profess with our lips. Jesus said, "This people honors Me with their lips, but their heart is far away from Me" (Matt. 15:8; Mark 7:6). If your spouse does not abandon you, then you are called to show him mercy.

Does that mean that the saved spouse has to withstand the abusive behavior of the other? I think not.

Many years ago John and I counseled a couple who professed to be Christians, but their marriage was in deep trouble. As we listened to the two of them, it became more and more obvious that she was vigorously hugging all the righteousness to herself and persistently attacking him, not only directly, but also throughout the community wherever anyone would give her audience. He acknowledged his sins and repented; she owned none.

During our devotional time the Holy Spirit led John and me to a scripture that leapt off the page to us:

There is a kind who is pure in his own eyes, yet is not washed from his filthiness. There is a kind—oh how lofty are his eyes! And his eyelids are raised in arrogance. There is a kind of man whose teeth are like swords, and his jaw teeth like knives, to devour the afflicted from the earth, and the needy from among men.

—PROVERBS 30:12–14

We exclaimed almost simultaneously, "That's it! There she is! Just change the pronouns—*her* eyes, *her* eyelids, *woman* whose teeth!"

Her husband was not only bleeding from her constant ripping and tearing, but he was also dying emotionally and spiritually, and his physical health was beginning to crumble. But he was determined to pursue reconciliation. We did all we could to help them both, but she would have none of it.

Finally he divorced her and remarried, this time to a woman who knew how to nurture his heart. The Lord, in His mercy, abundantly blessed their relationship, finances, health, and the ministry into which He had called them.

What ever happened to his ex-wife? Last we knew, she was still convinced that she was the only righteous one in the history of their relationship and that God would eventually bring her husband back to her!

Would it have been God's will to restore this marriage? Of course. But in a case such as this, where one partner relentlessly and unrepentantly persists in aggressive, destructive behavior that literally destroys the life of the other, and refuses to repent of any wrongdoing, reconciliation may be rendered impossible. God will not violate anyone's free will. God may, however, express His mercy and deliver the sincerely repented wounded one from the war zone.

## DID THE WEDDING EVER BECOME A MARRIAGE?

Vows may have been mouthed in the wedding ceremony, but has a one-flesh marriage become reality? Has the husband cut free from the bondage of parental allegiances that are no longer appropriate? Or is he now in a spiritually adulterous relationship with his parents, while blindly and stubbornly defending his position?

Jesus quotes from Genesis 2:24, saying, "For this cause a man shall leave his father and mother, and shall cleave to his wife; and the two shall become one flesh" (Matt. 19:5). Suppose that cleaving has never been accomplished because the prerequisite of leaving has never happened? Leaving necessarily precedes cleaving.

I have listened to the woeful tales of a number of women who have lived for years with "husbands" who either had never had sexual relations with their wives, or they did so only for a short time after the wedding and then fled from intimacy altogether.

These women had pursued previous counseling for themselves, but their "mates" stubbornly refused to acknowledge that there was a problem. The women were deeply wounded because they bore the title of "Mrs." but in reality were only cooks, housekeepers, hostesses, dinner companions, and laundresses. They felt belittled, rejected, and used, yet legally bound in what had never been a marriage.

So what was their reason for remaining in such a relationship? All too often I heard, "Because I am afraid of what he might do." Or, "Because he is well thought of in our town, and I'm afraid of what people might think of me." "Because my church teaches against divorce and I'd be condemned." "Because I'm afraid I might lose my salvation."

## MARRIED FOR THE WRONG REASONS

Sometimes very young girls marry for the wrong reasons. They leave home in rebellion, fleeing in hurt, fear, and confusion. They have no idea what might wait for them out there in the world, but the excruciatingly familiar abuse they have suffered at home can no longer be tolerated. They run—and continue running—to the point of exhaustion and futility.

Where can a penniless thirteen-year-old obtain something to eat and a place to sleep? How can she sustain herself without a job? She is convinced that nothing could be as bad as what she has left behind. Returning home is unthinkable. But she is hungry, cold, and very much alone.

What defense does she have against the pimps? The drug dealers? Any other kind of opportunist? She has no developed discernment to identify and reject trouble in unfamiliar forms, no maturity to enable her to project into the future and weigh the possible results of her decisions.

Her emotions are in chaos. She is easy prey for anyone offering any kind of tangible comfort. If she finds a man who seems to make reasonable promises to care for her, she may attach herself to him out of need; she may even marry him at some point. Suppose then that she later discovers she has latched on to more of a nightmare than the one she ran from in the first place. Would our loving and compassionate God hold her to that marriage covenant forever?

Sue* was thirteen when she left the nightmare she had lived in at home to follow a dream and a promise.

When Sue was only two years old, her mother had "gone away" and never returned. Sue could hardly remember her,

---

* Not her real name

and no one would talk about what had happened. Her father was an often-violent alcoholic. Her brothers were angry and abusive with no one to stop them.

Occasionally, when things became more than she could bear, she would manage to slip away and take a long walk around the neighborhood, though she knew she was sure to be punished when she returned. Sometimes she dreamed about living in someone else's home.

She had noticed other children playing happily in their yards who would sometimes be called in for cookies or other treats. She never knew what would happen when a member of her family opened the back door to call her name. She wished she had a friend she could talk to.

One day she walked by a man's house who lived several blocks away. He noticed this sad little girl who would walk past his house; often he stopped what he was doing to talk to her. For Sue, he seemed to be everything her father wasn't— understanding and compassionate—and for a little while she didn't feel so alone and afraid. In time, he befriended her, and Sue began to pour out her heart to him.

Eventually this man invited her to move away to another city, and, with no one to prevent her from leaving, she followed. And then reality began to hit her. Once again she was an object of abuse, and soon she became a mother. She stayed with him in a common-law situation for more than eighteen years.

During those years he began to drink more often, becoming increasingly abusive and violent, just like her father. She became fearful for her two daughters who remained at home. Seeking help through the church, she developed a relation-ship with the Lord. Over a period of time, she gained enough inner strength and self-esteem to stand up and say "no" to her common-law husband, and she left him.

She studied to earn her GED and did a creditable job of struggling to provide a home for her girls. There was never enough money to cover all their physical needs, but there seemed to be much more safety in poverty than she had known in the relationship from which she had fled.

Later Sue developed a love relationship with a man who asked her to marry him. After a time of testing and Christian counsel, she did. But he was a divorced man. Some of the legalists in her church quickly pointed fingers at their relationship, without concern about her history of abuse and not taking the time to understand the circumstances out of which either person had come.

## A CALL FOR COMPASSION

Jesus said, "What therefore God has joined together, let no man separate" (Matt. 19:6). Did God join anyone *together* in such a case? Some words were said as a formal entrance into what didn't become the kind of relationship God has in mind for a man and a woman. The Lord in His wisdom may know that there is no hope for change.

I strongly believe that God Himself can (and surely *may*) choose, in His mercy, to put asunder what men and women in their naïveté or foolishness have only thought to put together. I would further suggest that when repentance is real and forgiveness has been given by the Lord, He may also grant His grace for new beginnings.

The words of the psalmist have settled as a comforting balm into countless broken hearts:

> Remember, O LORD, Thy compassion and Thy lovingkind-
> nesses, for they have been from of old. Do not remember

the sins of my youth or my transgressions; according to
Thy lovingkindness remember Thou me, for Thy goodness' sake, O LORD.

—PSALM 25:6–7

I believe Jesus is still speaking the same words to the
Pharisees as He did two thousand years ago: "But go and learn
what this means, *'I desire compassion, and not sacrifice,'* for I
did not come to call the righteous, but sinners" (Matt. 9:13,
emphasis added).

There are many other situations that call for compassion.
For example, what about the wife whose husband hid from
her—and the children—his homosexual tendencies? Suddenly
she finds herself alone because he has decided to come out
openly about his gay lifestyle and no longer desires to be
married. What is she to do?

Or what about the couple who was heavily into drugs and
now the wife is a Christian and turned from that lifestyle,
but her husband continues to abuse drugs? Must she stay in
that abusive lifestyle? Worse yet, what if there are children
involved? Does she stay because, after all, the children need a
father, even if he is a drug addict?

If we are going to call ourselves Christians, we must be
careful to meet each individual as a person for whom Christ
died. It is fitting to realize that were it not for the grace of God
in our lives, we might well be suffering even as they are. We
must not allow ourselves to form hard opinions concerning
them from what appears on the surface of their lives. If we
live and pray in Jesus' name, we can never judge another with
condemnation. We must not fall into the pharisaical error
of making blanket statements concerning people who have
suffered the devastating pain of divorce.

On the other hand, I am not going to make blanket procla-
mations of mercy that would preclude anyone's own necessary
soul-searching. "Only, as the Lord has assigned to each one, as
God has called each, in this manner let him walk. And this I
direct in all the churches" (1 Cor. 7:17).

Please do not misunderstand me. I do warn everyone not to
take the laws of God lightly; He holds us accountable. I urge all
to pray for wisdom, discernment, and trust to recognize and
accept God's best will.

## STARTING OVER

If your husband has rejected you for another woman, or simply
for irreconcilable differences, don't allow yourself to become
caught in the bondage of super-intensive trying, by whatever
means, to get him back. Perhaps the Holy Spirit has told you to
pray diligently for reconciliation. Respond obediently. Contest
his action—especially if you have children. He may not even
begin to know his own mind. But I caution you against setting
all your hopes on your husband's return as though your very
life depended on it. Some women have persisted in this direction to the point of idolatry and insufferable manipulation.

Some women have even continued to battle in prayer,
though the divorced husband has long since remarried and
fathered children with his new wife. Now there are innocent
young children to consider. Issues become very complicated,
and there is no clearly moral way out, even though the letter of
the Law might declare *you* the righteous one.

Be assured that, whether your marriage is restored at some
future date or not, the Lord will never abandon you as a person.
He has a perfect plan and a meaningful purpose for you that
He never forgets.

You may not yet know what it is, "but seek first His kingdom and His righteousness; and all these things shall be added to you" (Matt. 6:33). The word *things* in this scripture refers specifically to food, drink, clothing—material provisions about which we are instructed not to be anxious. I believe that godly supply for emotional and spiritual needs also attends our seeking after His kingdom and His righteousness.

I implore you not to try to be your own counselor. You are not in a position to have clear, unbiased perspectives concerning your own problems. Pray to find someone who will draw your thoughts out, who will listen with a compassionate ear, discuss and advise without controlling, and pray with you about all your issues.

It is important for you to find out what the possible roots of dysfunction are in yourself that may have contributed to the breakdown of your marriage or the prevention of its healing. You need to discover what factors operating in you may have caused you to be blind so that you chose wrongly.

If you continue to see with unchanged eyes, you could possibly repeat the same mistakes. The Lord, through His cross, wants to set you free from the past and cause you to grow into all He created you to be, including the ability to participate fully in wholesome, healthy relationships—perhaps later on with another man.

Look for a church that has a small support group structure in which you can develop a sense of belonging to a family. Give yourself opportunity to make new friends who will love you unconditionally, encourage and nurture you, advise and confront you with no condemnation, and provide for you when you have special needs. Enter that structure also with a determination to give yourself to serve others.

Know that God Himself loves you unconditionally and eternally. You don't have to deserve or earn His love, and you can't lose it. Even His discipline is for your good.

> He *disciplines us* for *our* good, that we may share His holiness. All discipline for the moment seems not to be joyful, but sorrowful; yet to those who have been trained by it, afterwards it yields the peaceful fruit of righteousness. Therefore, strengthen the hands that are weak and the knees that are feeble, and make straight paths for your feet, so that *the limb* which is lame may not be put out of joint, but rather be healed.
> —HEBREWS 12:10–13, *emphasis added*

The Lord's desire is not to punish you for your mistakes, but rather to discipline you in love so that you don't unwittingly repeat those same errors. His desire is to redeem your mistakes and restore you to wholeness.

What about the questions (listed at the beginning of this chapter) that plague you?

1. *You made a bad choice?* Can you trust your judgment again? God will not only forgive your mistakes, but He is also able to redeem them. You can trust His ability to purify and transform your judgment. But He needs your invitation and cooperation.

2. *You can't face being alone for the rest of your life?* Don't be in a hurry to fill the void. God's arms are the only safe ones to rush into. When the news of your divorce becomes public, the predators will try to close in on you. Some know they

are taking advantage of your vulnerability and will do it anyway without conscience. Others are seeking solace or affirmation for themselves. They will unwittingly do it at your expense, pressuring you into sexual relationships, though they may have convinced themselves they only want to help you. Don't jeopardize what God may have planned for your future by grabbing something cheap to comfort you in your present moment of pain. Such comfort does away with your pain like poison gas.

3. *You are afraid of your own neediness?* Good! Tell God about it. Talk with a trusted friend.

4. *What do you do with your sexual drive?* Sex in the aftermath of a divorce can be one of the most confusing, defiling, and eventually humiliating experiences of your life. Don't be ashamed of your sexual drive. You are alive! You are also single now. (See the section about sex and singles in the previous chapter.)

5. *You feel unattractive?* Your body is a temple of the Holy Spirit (1 Cor. 6:19). God's temple is beautiful. Pray to see yourself with His eyes.

6. *Old friends uncomfortable around you?* Choose to forgive. Busy yourself with things you like to do. Make new friends. The old ones, if they are genuine, will come back eventually. Remember that they too are hurting and just don't know what to do or say.

7. *How can you minister to your children?* Talk to them. They need to hear that *your* divorce is not *their* fault. Ask their forgiveness for failures and fractures. You don't have to say it is all your fault; it may not be. Don't make disparaging remarks about your ex-husband. As bad as he may have been, remember that he is still their father. They need to know you are deeply sorry for their sake that you were not able to maintain a secure, two-parent family environment for them.

Assure them you will never leave them. Share with them quality times that include recreation. Give them compliments and copious affection appropriate to their age level. Do not fail in the least of your promises to them.

If you are going to be late arriving home from work, call them and let them know about it. They need the security of knowing where you are and that you are concerned for them. Encourage them to talk about their feelings. Assure them that it is OK to be angry, to be afraid.

Teach them by your example constructive ways of handling emotions like anger and fear. Pray with them, honestly expressing feelings, calling for God's comfort and strength, and confirming His loving presence with you (whether you feel it or not). Play with them. Life is heavy now, and the atmosphere can be lightened for you and them if you can regularly do fun things together.

8. *Pray for a good job, good health, and the humility to ask for help when you need it.* You may have to

make severe financial adjustments that require prioritizing issues you have never had to deal with before. But the children will find their security much more in your personal loving attention and nurture than in material provisions. Don't sacrifice their emotional and spiritual welfare for a job that takes you away from them too much.

9. *It is not of primary importance what people think of you.* It is extremely important what God thinks of you. But He already knows you better than you know yourself and is able to judge the thoughts and intentions of your heart with merciful understanding.

Whether you are separated, going through a divorce, or are now divorced, know that you have a High Priest who sympathizes with your weaknesses (Heb. 4:15). You can boldly approach the throne of grace and find mercy. He knows that raising your children alone is no small feat, and He will be there to support you every step of the way. As a mother, your greatest days are ahead. You have been given the greatest calling ever known; treasure these years.

*Chapter 10*

# A MOTHER'S
# HEARTACHES

**M**OTHERHOOD HAS ALWAYS BEEN a tremendous privilege (and responsibility) that brings, I believe, joys and rewards that far outweigh possible difficulties and sorrows. As a mother, you will never in any other circumstance have an opportunity to influence the life of another human being so profoundly as you do your own child.

You will not experience the quality of satisfaction and deeply rooted exhilaration you receive as you watch your offspring grow to maturity with understanding and skills that surpass your own. Raising a child in the loving, life-giving nurture and discipline of the Lord is a sacred trust and an eternal work. There is no more important calling or anointing on the life of anyone.

Yet with this enormous task comes tremendous responsibility. In this present generation, emotional and spiritual responsibilities of parents have become awesome and frightening because of the increasingly powerful, seductive, and defiling influences from our deteriorating culture that press in upon our children. While they are still babes, we can maintain some control over their environment.

Early parental problems have to do largely with diapers and toilet training, runny noses, bumps and bruises, eating, sleeping, cleaning up messes, and discovering what sort of discipline is appropriate to the little person who must learn freedom within safe and healthy parameters.

Frustrations begin to arise when that little one starts to push those boundaries and to express resistance, sometimes emphatically, when we veto unsupervised exploration of rooms, drawers, and toilet bowls. We often find ourselves chuckling at the cute things they do or say.

But when your children begin, as they must, to experience life in the company of their peers, anxieties begin to well up in your heart because, as a parent, you care. Will the deposit of love and training you have put into your offspring be enough to enable them to resist the force of negative outside influences?

## INCREASED ANXIETIES WITHIN OUR CHANGING CULTURE

When my husband and I were raising our family, we were very much concerned about the foul language our children heard from others in our neighborhood, but the potty-mouths were in the minority. Expressions of profanity and filth were relatively limited and pale by today's standards.

Today such speech has become so commonplace that in the general populace few seem to be offended. And if you openly express your objections, you become ridiculed as being a "religious fanatic" or a "Bible-thumper."

Not too many years ago television pro[...] movies were still subject to some rather strict cens[...] [ac]tors and actresses still wore pajamas in bedroom sc[...] intimate interludes were left largely to the imaginati[...] a family begins to enjoy what they think is a whole[...] [mo]vie and suddenly find themselves viewing a pornogra[...] [episo]de that has little to do with the plot.

In previous generations, mischief was a [...] part of growing up, but deliberately destructive vandali[...] almost unheard of. For instance, it was a fairly comm[...] [occu]rrence on a weekend for someone to wake up to fin[...] lawn creatively toilet-papered by a group of partying te[...]s, but school properties were not wantonly destroyed by[...] and twelve-year-old delinquents.

Schoolteachers were still given authority to [disci]pline their students, even with a supervised paddling [in m]any schools. Some parents may have complained, but [in m]any homes parental discipline supported and reinforce[d sch]ool discipline.

Most children go through a period of fascinati[on w]ith lighting matches, which sometimes accidentally get[s out] of hand. Our son Johnny once set the corner of his beds[h...] on fire, and Tim started a more serious blaze in the basem[...] of the parsonage where we lived, but both boys had the pre[sen]ce of mind to quench the flames before much damage was [don]e. They also accepted the disciplinary consequences of [the]ir adventures and learned from their experiences.

Young boys used to play cops-and-robbers in backya[rd]s, alleys, and vacant lots. It was only a game, and they would t[ak]e turns being the "good guys," who were usually the winne[rs]. Today we read reports in our newspapers concerning youn[g] people who have brought real firearms to school and childr[en]

who have act / their playmates, teachers, or parents.
Unmanageab / es are increasing in the world today,
and restraint / g.

Very few / ople in previous generations grew up
without at l / trying cigarettes (or homemade facsim-
iles) and be / e time our children reached their teens,
some drug / marijuana, were easily available, but not
yet to grad / children. Now, young people can exper-
iment just / ith drugs like crack cocaine and become
instantly / d. We have to watch our street corners and
alleys car / or pushers. And many children don't have to
go outsi / own homes for a ready supply of alcoholic
beverage

Forni / used to be considered a sin. Now there is a push
to prom / afe sex" as a means of protecting our children. I
apprec / e intent to protect, but what a lie this communicates t / children!

Qui / ide from the very real (but frequently ignored,
denie / minimized) moral and sociological implications
invol / n promiscuity, there is a *fact* that should be presented
boldl / d clearly to our young people. Condoms are *not* and
neve / ve been guarantors of safe sex. They fail in varieties of
way / d many people living today were conceived as a result
of ti / e failures.

H / the development and use of newer and more sophisti-
cat / means of birth control caused us to forget so completely
th / we can, with few or no pangs of conscience, communicate
to / ur young people a false security?

As I write, I remind myself that this is supposed to be a
book concerning the *healing* of a woman's emotions. Now I'm
beginning to feel rather emotional myself as I identify with
the grief and anxiety of mothers everywhere who see their

children, especially teenagers, sucked into the stream of our polluted and seductive culture and are too often overcome by it.

We begin to experience a sense of helplessness to protect or retrieve our "babies" from the flood that threatens to destroy their lives. Please don't despair. I *will* turn to a more positive and healing note. But first it is helpful to understand how we arrived in such a cultural predicament and to become aware of popular "solutions" that are not likely to be adequate.

## WHAT CAUSED THIS MESS?

One of the reasons why we are seeing an erosion of values in our society is because too many children have become orphans (whether emotionally or physically), largely due to wars that took their fathers away from home and claimed the lives of many. When the wars ended, great numbers of those who returned were emotionally wounded or occupied with catching up with schooling and careers—to the extent that their children did not receive quality time and attention. Therefore, lacking adequate relationship and modeling for themselves, many men today have never known how to be nurturing and disciplining fathers. Some have abdicated their position unconsciously from ignorance, and others consciously from frustration and fear.

Another reason is that respect for the absolute and eternal laws of God has been eroded. The image we develop of God the Father is significantly shaped and colored at the heart level by what we experienced with our natural fathers.

If your father did not cherish and protect you, then the question arises, why should Father God? If your father rejected and abandoned you physically or emotionally, then you will expect Father God to do the same. If your father abused you, then you will tend to see God as being harsh and unfair. If your father was never there for you, then you probably have difficulty believing that God is real. If your father was present physically but emotionally distant and never disciplined you, then you will be unable to believe that God will hold you accountable in love.

Those who have been seriously wounded in any way by their natural fathers will be extremely vulnerable to humanistic voices advocating a kind of moral and spiritual anarchy that discounts the eternal laws of God and proclaims every person to be his or her own god. In this new system "my feelings" masquerade as truth, and "my needs" take priority over honesty and over the welfare of the whole family or other corporate groups.

Divorce rates, which have risen radically, have also contributed to this confusion. Thousands of mothers (and an increasing number of fathers) are trying to raise children in single-parent homes, usually under tremendous stress.

Even though you may be doing an admirable job, God never intended you to do double duty; He did not equip you to be both mother *and* father. Single parents are crying out for help. Even though the Bible says again and again to care for the orphans, few churches or other organizations are structured to fulfill the needs of such a rapidly growing segment of our society.

## THE PARENTING DILEMMA

Many young married couples, wounded and intimidated by what they personally experienced, are making decisions not to have children because they don't want the "terrible" responsibility of raising them in a world such as this.

Teenagers are having abortions with no conviction that they are committing murder, for which they will eventually reap. And so-called "enlightened authorities" are persuading them with lies that there is really no moral issued involved.

Conversely, increasing numbers of teenagers and young women are giving birth to babies when they haven't the foggiest understanding of what it means to be a parent. They are at a naturally self-centered stage of their own development and haven't the maturity to be able to sacrifice their own comfort or desire consistently for the sake of their babies.

Whatever their reason for becoming pregnant, they aren't aware that the motivating power for their affection is not first to bless the baby but to comfort themselves. Unless there are family members to support these child-mothers until they grow up, they often neglect, abuse, and/or abandon their babies.

Many people who have chosen to raise families have substantial reasons to fear for their children, because they themselves lack the knowledge, experience, and wisdom necessary to provide the quality of love and discipline to build a sturdy foundation and secure family structure. They cannot model or communicate what they never received. Now, as problems arise, many are attempting too late, with anxiety and urgency, to seek help to equip themselves.

Others have become so pressured to maintain a certain standard of living, so consumed with building a career, or so busy with personal interests outside the home that they have simply failed to spend quality time sharing themselves with their children.

Without realizing it, they have trained their sons and daughters from their earliest years to look first or only outside the home environment for meaningful relationships, affirmation, and answers to life's problems. Panic eventually hits, and they cry, "How could my children turn their backs on me when I have given them everything?" Every *thing*, yes, but *no real relationship with a primary person.*

## UNDERSTANDING TEENS AND TRUSTING GOD WITH THEM

Too few Christians have enough faith in the overcoming power of Jesus Christ to trust God with the deposit of training and moral values they have seeded into the lives of their children. They tend to try too hard to control and protect their teenagers just at the time when it is appropriate to cut them free emotionally. Teens are necessarily in the process of *individuating* and establishing their *independence.*

They must, as they move into adulthood, say, "I am me. I am not you. I am my own person, and I have an opinion of my own." It is impossible for them to jump successfully from a child's position in the family, where all decisions are made for them, to an adult position in which they are suddenly expected to manage their own lives.

So-called "model children" who, two weeks after they have left home to enroll in the university, suddenly flip out are repeated testimony to that reality. The teen years need to be a time of transitional learning during which young people are considered to be adults, responsible before God for their own mistakes (a very biblical concept).

During this time a wise parent becomes a coach. He involves the teenager in the development of home rules for considerate living, and together they work out fair penalties for violations. Parents hold teenagers accountable for what has been agreed upon, and they watch their own behavior so as not to model contrary values.

Teenagers desperately need parents who listen, who believe in them when they may be as yet insecure and unable to believe in themselves. They need their parents to trust them even when they can't be trusted. The home doors must be left open to the prodigal as parents watch prayerfully, so that when they come to themselves, their senses, as in Luke 15:17, they have a place to return to—loved ones who will receive them compassionately.

Teens are also involved in an essential natural process of accomplishing what we call *internalization*. They will and they must examine everything they have been taught, test many things, and come to decisions about what they will call their own. This is a large part of the reason they are so self-centered during this period of their lives. They are necessarily working on themselves.

Many parents don't understand what is going on, and even those who do, usually find teens difficult to live with patiently. But if anxious parents panic and push, treat them as children rather than as budding adults, or respond to questioning and testing with consistent criticism, teenagers perceive that parents have all the ground of righteousness occupied.

In order to be their own person, teens feel compelled to take an opposite stance, even though it may not be what they really want. In the midst of the battle that ensues, Christian parents then often drive teenagers beyond normal, healthy individuation into *rebellion*. When rebellion has taken hold of young people, they become vulnerable to every prevailing stronghold in our culture.

## WHO'S TO BLAME?

I am not saying that parents are to blame for all of the rebellious sins of their children. Why? First, at some point in every person's life he/she must take responsibility for his/her own responses. Second, in today's world we are surrounded by increasing confusion and wickedness. Much of it comes wrapped in attractive packages through television programming and the Internet. Even if your children don't see it at home, they will be exposed to it to some extent in someone else's home.

A good deal of it is presented in the guise of enlightened knowledge and practical, scientific authority by godless ones who have infiltrated our educational system. In many places and ways, these humanists wield significant influence.

You can substitute with home schooling, but eventually your child will have to go out and associate with other people. Will his/her education be experientially adequate to prepare him/her to interact successfully with the people of the world? Will you send your child to Christian schools? A good Christian school may help, but many of the students in Christian schools are not yet Christian. In fact, some of them are there because they have problems that the public schools cannot handle.

Much of the world's confusion is passed on to our children by the other children with whom they associate. Children naturally want to be accepted among their peers, and they will be vulnerable to the attitudes and values of their friends. It is becoming increasingly difficult for a child to find a friend today who does not come from a dysfunctional family.

Some families are so dysfunctional they don't even recognize they have problems. Parents, no matter how hard they try, cannot altogether prevent their offspring from negative and harmful influences. They can, however, provide them with equipment to live with strength in the midst of a wicked and perverse generation, to stand and to be in (but not of) the world. Much of the equipment is built into a child by simple acts.

## What You Can Do as a Mother

All hope is not lost. There are things that you can do to build strength into your child at every stage of development in his or her life.

*While your baby is in your womb, pray daily for protection and blessing, and that he or she would feel welcomed.*

Listen to melodious music. From conception, your baby has a sensitive personal spirit, or there would be no life in his or her little body (James 2:26). While your child is in the womb, he or she has the capacity to experience, receive, and respond. If you faithfully voice the prayers, it is God's job to make something happen. Ask your husband to speak a father's blessing. Insofar as it is possible, stay out of tension-producing situations. Do not smoke, drink alcohol, or take drugs. Eat a nourishing diet, and get regular exercise and plenty of rest.

*Breast-feed your baby if possible.*

If you have trouble, consult La Leche League or WIC (Women, Infants, and Children nutrition program) for helpful instruction. If for some reason beyond your control you use a bottle, be sure to cuddle your baby while feeding.

You are not just pouring milk into your baby; you are pouring love.

### Hold and tenderly rock your baby.

Talk and sing to him or her. Babies comprehend much more with their sensitive little spirits than they do with their minds. You cannot spoil a child with warm, wholesome, affectionate touch. By showing your child affection, you *will* build in a basic trust that he or she is chosen and precious, and he or she will settle into a secure sense of belonging.

### Change your baby's diapers—even the messy ones—with joy.

Be delighted with the privilege! By this you will teach him or her to accept, appreciate, and respect natural body functions. Your attitude influences the baby's sexuality. Build into your baby quiet expectations to be comforted and not shamed.

### Encourage your husband to participate in caring for the baby.

Your husband is the primary person to receive and carry the baby away from the familiar territory of mother. If his arms are strong and gentle, the baby will begin to develop positive anticipation of the world away from you and security apart from you. It is the primary task of the father to draw the child forth into life. Proper nurture from a mother and a father give the baby courage to be, to adventure and risk, and to meet other people vulnerably, spirit to spirit. If your husband resists becoming involved, check your anger and give it to the Lord. God can handle your negative emotions; your baby would be wounded and confused by them.

*Enjoy each stage of your child's development.*

Take time to play with your child. Laugh with your child. A simple game of peek-a-boo teaches your baby that though you may disappear, you will surely return. Little children delight in repetition of experiences that write comfort and reassurance on their hearts.

*Leave your child with a reliable babysitter once in a while.*

Your husband needs to have some romantic time just with you, and this also teaches your little one that, though you may leave for a while, you have not abandoned him or her. However, do not leave your child with a sitter so much that he or she feels forsaken and begins to look to the sitter as the primary caregiver. Don't forfeit your privilege of motherhood. No one can adequately replace you. If it is absolutely necessary for you to work and leave your child in some sort of day care, be careful to spend consistent, quality time with him or her at the end of each day. Tell your child, "I missed you! I am so glad to see you!" Tell him or her with words, hugs, and participation in activities that you both enjoy.

*As your son or daughter develops, read stories, work, and play together.*

Encourage, compliment, listen, teach with patience, and give appropriate hugs and kisses. Let discipline be applied consistently with love, never with condemnation.

*Be an example to your child on how to pray.*

God is compassionately interested in your child's personal issues whether it's skinned knees, bruises, disappointments, or hurt feelings. He understands our fears and does not ridicule our tears. As problems and feelings arise, train your child to talk to the Lord simply and directly about them.

Share also your joys and gratitude together, giving thanks to God for His loving presence, protection, and provision. *You are a living epistle. You represent God to your child.*

### Don't stifle your children's sense of adventure.

As they become older and begin to venture into the neighborhood, pray for their protection, and let them go. Arm them with some commonsense understanding, but do not become overprotective. How will they learn the meaning of comfort and healing if they are never allowed to stumble and fall? How will they learn the delightful refreshment of a warm bath if they are not allowed to get dirty? Hold them accountable for mistakes with firm and fair discipline—for their good, not to make them behave so *you* can look good. Communicate the message, "I love you too much to let you get away with this." Never excommunicate them from your love. Be warmly available.

### Give older children room to grow.

When your children become teenagers, remember what I wrote earlier in this chapter and cut them totally free from you in prayer. In the flesh, you want to emotionally bind your children to you. But then they could not become their own person with their own center of decision. When you're tempted to give unsolicited advice, bite your tongue. When they do ask for your advice, tell them less than what you would like to say. Give them the opportunity to draw information from you. Listen to their opinions, and try not to register too much shock or alarm; they may only be testing you. Hear them out.

***Pray for the protection of your children at every level of their development.***

Especially when they are in their teens, stand with them in spiritual warfare against the forces of darkness in the world that would press in to threaten, seduce, attack, oppress, or push them in any way. Command those forces to stand back in the name of Jesus.

Then pray for your children that they be strengthened in their own inner man, in their own spirit, to make their own righteous decisions:

> For this reason, I bow my knees before the Father, from whom every family in heaven and on earth derives its name, that He would grant you, according to the riches of His glory, *to be strengthened with power through His Spirit in the inner man;* so that Christ may dwell in your hearts through faith; and that you, being rooted and grounded in love, may be able to comprehend with all the saints what is the breadth and length and height and depth, and to know the love of Christ which surpasses knowledge, that you may be filled up with all the fullness of God.
> —EPHESIANS 3:14–19, *emphasis added*

Travail for them in prayer as Paul spoke of in Galatians 4:19. You are again pregnant, in a spiritual sense, with their life until Christ is formed in them. Carry them in your heart (Phil. 1:7). You must not try to control them, or you will drive them away from you, from the good values you have tried to instill in them during their formative years, and from the Lord.

### *Trust God to care for them.*

As you begin to give your children more freedom to take responsibility for their own lives, trust God and the deposit of love and nurture that have been built into them. Or, if you know those virtues to be seriously lacking in their foundations, make a decision to trust God's redemptive power.

## FOR THE SINGLE MOM

If you are a single parent, accept for yourself these words spoken to Israel:

> "For your husband is your Maker, whose name is the LORD of hosts; and your Redeemer is the Holy One of Israel, who is called the God of all the earth. For the LORD has called you, like a wife forsaken and grieved in spirit, even like a wife of one's youth when she is rejected," says your God.
>
> —ISAIAH 54:5–6

You can rest in God and trust Him when parenting becomes overwhelming. Begin by reminding yourself that your children are, first of all, a gift from God (Ps. 127:3). God's Word is full of promises that He will take care of you and your children. God will:

- Provide wisdom, knowledge, understanding, and protection for those who walk in His integrity (Prov. 2:6–7).

- Gird you with strength (Ps. 18:32).

- Answer your prayers (Matt. 21:22).

ల్ల    Supply all your needs (Phil. 4:19).

God promises to be a father to the fatherless (Ps. 68:5), providing justice, food, and clothing (Deut. 10:18; 14:29). In times of trouble He is a very present help (Ps. 46:1). Even if something were to happen to you, God will take responsibility for your children (Ps. 27:10).

Your weeping will not last forever (Ps. 30:5). So "be anxious for nothing, but in everything by prayer and supplication with thanksgiving let your requests be made known to God. And the peace of God, which surpasses all comprehension, shall guard your hearts and your minds in Christ Jesus" (Phil. 4:6–7).

## You Are a Work in Progress

Are you walking around under a load of guilt because you see your children in trouble and feel that you have failed miserably as a mother? Do you think that God did not know that you would make mistakes? He knew exactly where, when, and how much you would fail, and He sent your children to you anyway. If you could have been a perfect mother, wouldn't your children have needed a Savior anyway? If you had been a perfect mother, do you believe your children would have given the perfect response? Not likely.

Everyone was created with free will; God did not want it any other way, because He does not want robots. He wants sons and daughters with whom He can fellowship. God is a perfect Father, yet all of His children except One need a Savior. There is not one who has not gone astray at some time. God is not therefore disqualified as a father because we (as His children) make mistakes. Jesus never sinned, but His disciples all failed Him, one of them to the extent of total betrayal. That does not disqualify Him to be the Lord of the universe. Nor do your children's failures disqualify you as a parent. It is not a reflection of your parenting.

You and I have not been perfect mothers, but most of us have done the best we know how. All of us have been maturing in the process, and though many of us are grandmothers, we are not yet all grown up. God loves us unconditionally and will not abandon us.

It is not our job to redeem the mistakes we have made with our children. That is the Lord's job. It is appropriate for us to repent and ask the Lord's and our children's forgiveness for all real and imagined guilt—and to *receive* forgiveness. Perhaps our children are not ready to forgive, but the Lord is. And it is His task to prepare their hearts. You need to quit wallowing in self-punishing attitudes and actions and get on with daily living and loving to the utmost of your present capacity—to allow the Lord to live and love in and through you.

A great deal of our children's healing comes as they relate, even remotely, to the process of healing in us. The more whole we become, the purer and more effective our prayers will be. Prayers of protection and blessing are appropriate even for our adult children.

You say you don't feel that you "deserve" to be forgiven? You're right. Nobody deserves God's forgiveness. But since the Lord has already died for your sins on the cross, why do you keep passing judgment on yourself and say you don't "deserve" to receive that for which He gave His life to make available to you? Perhaps you know the Lord forgives you, but you just can't forgive yourself. If so, you have just installed yourself on a throne higher than God's. God will let us wallow in self-condemnation as long as we choose, but it is the antithesis of His nature and produces no good fruit whatsoever. Reprogram yourself to receive His forgiveness, knowing that He has redeemed you and will restore you to wholeness once again.

## REDEEMED AND RESTORED

How can you have faith to believe that God is able to redeem your mistakes? Isaiah 51:3 promises that God will comfort all our waste places and make our wildernesses like Eden and our deserts like the garden of the Lord. Of course, the Bible is full of examples, but let me share with you an example of God's redeeming power.

### Breaking free

When we first met Jane*, she was one of those young women about whom you find yourself thinking, *She could be really beautiful if she would lose about fifty pounds.* Our hearts broke for her as she poured out her feelings of low self-esteem and loneliness, the hopelessness she had concerning her future, and the despair she felt concerning any possibility of experiencing significant change.

Jane's parents had divorced, and she was living with her extremely bitter and possessive mother who relentlessly poured out a vitriolic stream of self-pity and resentment against her former husband. Jane had no boyfriend, no social life, and little opportunity to develop friendships. Though she had great undeveloped musical ability, she worked steadily as a custodian in a large public building, where she specialized in cleaning toilets.

---

\* Not her real name

After counseling with Jane for several weeks, we began to talk with her about her future. We suggested that she go back to school to develop her musical talent or whatever else her heart yearned for. We talked with her about scholarships and other financial aids. But we kept running up against a wall of futility in her.

It then became apparent to us that she had accepted the lie that she shouldn't dare leave her hurting mother—that somehow her mother's welfare depended on her remaining at home. She felt compelled to sacrifice her life to be her mother's rock and emotional refuge. We, and her father, had to persist patiently in prayer and conversation with her before she was able to recognize that she had been emotionally manipulated and had finally become a prisoner of delusion.

Despite her mother's loud protests, she was finally able to cut free. She enrolled in a university far from her home, pursued her musical training, graduated with honors, lost more than fifty pounds, and married a fine Christian man.

Without her, Jane's mother did not die—not even to her own self-centered attitudes—and certainly not to her anger toward us as the ones who persuaded her daughter to break free. But God isn't finished with her yet.

The importance of this story is to say that even though a misguided mother may travail with sinful motivations for all the wrong purposes, God is still able to rescue His children, set them on the right course, and bring them into the glory He has prepared for them.

## HOPE FOR TODAY AND TOMORROW

It certainly appears that dysfunctional families are becoming the norm, and the lives of few children are being built on foundations without serious fractures. At the same time, the Lord is pouring His Holy Spirit upon *all* mankind (Joel 2:28), not just Christians. This means that people everywhere are hungrily searching for spiritual realities to comfort their hearts and fill their emptiness, and not only for intellectual answers to problems. Many are receiving Jesus as Lord and Savior, and the Holy Spirit comes to dwell within their hearts.

But some who have become disillusioned with the Christian church, and many who are unloved, untaught, and undisciplined, are extremely vulnerable and, without discernment, are searching in New Age philosophies and occultism. When they feed on Satan's counterfeits that cannot satisfy, they tend to crave more because they have swallowed the lying promise of belonging, fulfillment, and power. Satan seems to be able to come up with enough deceptive spiritual titillations to keep them on the hook.

Yet there are thousands of jean-clad young people who are flocking to churches that present the gospel through a contemporary style of music in worship that communicates a clear "Jesus-now-His-Presence-with-me-and-His-Spirit-living-in-me" message of hope. They are unwilling to settle with going through the motions of being Christian or playing games. They want to be accepted just as they are into a *family* that offers unconditional nurturing love. They long to experience the power of a living God to change lives.

The church is called to be an organism of family groups in which individual members lay down their lives for one another so that each person may receive the nurturing foundation that their natural family was unequipped to provide. This is what Paul was praying for:

> So that Christ may dwell in your hearts through faith;
> and that you, *being rooted and grounded in love*, may be
> able to comprehend with all the saints what is the breadth
> and length and height and depth, and to know the love of
> Christ which surpasses knowledge, that you may be filled
> up to all the fulness of God.
> —EPHESIANS 3:17–19, *emphasis added*

With that quality of foundational preparation, the church is called to go into all the world and preach the gospel. And we are seeing many of these wounded ones being healed by God's grace, revelation, and power. But there is often such a depth of hurt and anxiety in them that, even after receiving the Lord, they need a great deal of prayer to prepare their hearts to accept and walk in their healing.

That is where you come in. Mothers! Travail for your children! Christians! Travail for your spiritual children! I invite you to consider the following scripture as a *rhema* word to you as a part of the body of Christ.

> "As soon as Zion travailed, she also brought forth her sons.
> Shall I bring to the point of birth, and not give delivery?"
> says the LORD. "Or shall I who gives delivery shut the
> womb?" says your God.
>
> "Be joyful with Jerusalem and rejoice for her, all you
> who love her; be exceedingly glad with her, all you who
> mourn over her, that you may nurse and be satisfied
> with her comforting breasts, that you may suck and be
> delighted with her bountiful bosom." For thus says the
> LORD, "Behold, I extend peace to her like a river, and the
> glory of the nations like an overflowing stream; and you
> shall be nursed, you shall be carried on the hip and fondled

on the knees. As one whom his mother comforts, so I will comfort you, and you shall be comforted in Jerusalem."

Then you shall see this, and your heart shall be glad, and your bones shall flourish like the new grass; and the hand of the LORD shall be made known to His servants, but He shall be indignant toward His enemies.

—ISAIAH 66:8–14

I am aware that the words *Zion* and *Jerusalem* in the Bible are believed by many to refer to the Jewish nation. Others insist that in some instances these names refer to the church. Others like myself believe that both views are correct in light of Romans 10:11–13:

> For the Scripture says, "Whoever believes in Him will not be disappointed." For there is no distinction between Jew and Greek; for the same Lord is Lord of all, abounding in riches for all who call upon Him; for "Whoever will call upon the name of the Lord will be saved."

As the body of Christ, we are called to be a nurturing body for broken families and a healing body for the nations. We must learn to carry others in our hearts and to travail in prayer for the children as Paul did (Gal. 4:19). Those children will then have opportunity to "grow up in all aspects into Him, who is the head, even Christ" (Eph. 4:15) and bring healing to many more.

As women, we are naturally equipped with faith and stamina for labor in childbirth. "Whenever a woman is in travail she has sorrow, because her hour has come; but when she gives birth to the child, she remembers the anguish no more, for joy that a child has been born into the world" (John 16:21). In ministry we need only to transfer what we know in the natural realm to the task we are called to do in the spiritual.

God has created women with a special gift of tenderness that nurtures. In 1 Thessalonians 2:6–7, Paul speaks of his ministry, along with Sylvanus and Timothy, having been successful largely because of the way they had chosen to emulate that gift rather than assert their authority. "But we proved to be gentle among you, as a nursing mother tenderly cares for her own children" (v. 7).

It is important that we remember that though there is no male or female in Christ (Gal. 3:28) (that is, we are all one in Him), there are many distinctly female attributes that we should cherish. Each of us will grow into the freedom to be and express all that we are when we can say, "Thank You, God, for making me *me*." And then we enter into a relationship with Him who is our primary source of love, hope, strength, affirmation, and peace.

# NOTES

## Chapter 2: Women's Liberation in the Bible

1. Rachel Levine, "The Biblical Woman," *YAVO Digest*, vol. 3, no. 6, p. 12. Used by permission. Copyright protected.

## Chapter 6: Mixed Signals—Learning to Handle Emotional Overload

1. Donald Joy interview, "The Innate Differences between Males and Females," *Focus on the Family* Radio Broadcast, CS-099, 1984, 1986.

## Chapter 7: Coping With a Loved One's Substance Abuse

1. "Living With an Alcoholic," ComPsych Corporation, 2002, http://www.maricopa.gov/Benefits/pdf/AA/Living_with_Alcoholic.pdf (accessed August 23, 2006).
2. Ibid.

3. U.S. Department of Health and Human Services and SAMHSA's National Clearing House for Alcohol and Drug Information, FAQs, http://ncadi.samhsa.gov/help/faq.aspx#substance (accessed August 23, 2006).

### Chapter 9: God's Mercy for the Divorcée

1. Fred H. Wight, *Manners and Customs of Bible Lands* (Chicago, IL: Moody Press, 1989), 125.

# OTHER BOOKS *by* JOHN *and* PAULA SANDFORD

*Transformation of the Inner Man*
*Healing the Wounded Spirit*
*Healing Victims of Sexual Abuse*
*Why Some Christians Commit Adultery*
*Renewal of the Mind*
*Choosing Forgiveness*
*Awakening the Slumbering Spirit*
*Restoring the Christian Family*

For further information, contact:

Elijah House, Inc.
317 N. Pines Road
Spokane Valley, WA 99206
Web site: www.elijahhouse.org

# JOHN and PAULA SANDFORD

### have devoted their lives to helping people make changes and walk out their victories.

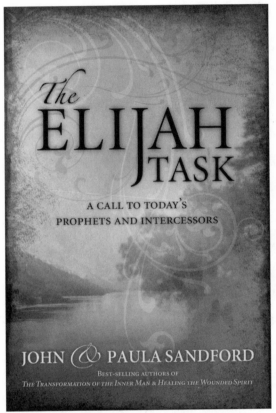

1-59979-020-3 / 978-1-59979-020-6 / $14.99

We know that you have found peace and comfort, and that God has been revealed in *Healing for a Woman's Emotions*. Here is another classic teaching from John and Paula Sandford.

### The Elijah Task

**It is time to see the task God has set before you!**

For prophets and intercessors who want a deeper understanding of their role in the world today (and for those who want to understand and support the prophets and intercessors), all of you have a mighty important job to do.

The spirit of Elijah is repentance, which brings change and great joy! There is much work to be done, and *The Elijah Task* is the perfect place to start.

### Visit your local bookstore today.

Charisma
HOUSE
A STRANG COMPANY

6656

# Strang Communications,

publisher of both **Charisma House** and *Charisma* magazine, wants to give you

# 3 FREE ISSUES

of our **award-winning** magazine.

Since its inception in 1975 *Charisma* magazine has helped thousands of Christians stay connected with what God is doing worldwide.

Within its pages you will discover in-depth reports and the latest news from a Christian perspective, biblical health tips, global events in the body of Christ, personality profiles, and so much more. Join the family of *Charisma* readers who enjoy feeding their spirits each month with miracle-filled testimonies and inspiring articles that bring clarity, provoke prayer, and demand answers.

To claim your **3 free issues** of *Charisma*, send your name and address to: Charisma 3 Free Issues Offer, 600 Rinehart Road, Lake Mary, FL 32746. Or you may call **1-800-829-3346** and ask for Offer # **96FREE**. This offer is only valid in the USA.

# Charisma
## +CHRISTIAN LIFE
www.charismamag.com

5567